Divided We Fall

Exploring the Keys to American Unity, Survival, and Prosperity

William W. Robé

iUniverse, Inc.
Bloomington

Divided We Fall
Exploring the Keys to American Unity, Survival, and Prosperity

iUniverse books may be ordered through booksellers or by contacting:

iUniverse
1663 Liberty Drive
Bloomington, IN 47403
www.iuniverse.com
1-800-Authors (1-800-288-4677)

ISBN: 978-1-4759-4297-2 (sc)
ISBN: 978-1-4759-4298-9 (hc)
ISBN: 978-1-4759-4299-6 (e)

Library of Congress Control Number: 2012914328

Printed in the United States of America

iUniverse rev. date: 9/6/2012

This book is dedicated to all
civil servants
(local, state, and federal)
who have put service before self-interest.

The author's net proceeds from this book will be donated
to the Alzheimer's Research Fund, supported by the
National Association of Retired Federal Employees (NARFE).

Contents

PART 3
Hopes and Aspirations 139

PART 4
Appendix 159

The author's statement before the US House of Representatives' Select Committee on Aging, held in Missoula, Montana, on April 17, 1983—followed by commentary.

Acknowledgments

The author would like to thank Al and Sylvia Cook for editing the original manuscript. Their keen eyes found many misplaced commas and other errors of punctuation. Their ability to detect the slightest of errors has earned my admiration and deepest appreciation.

My thanks also go out to the many mentors in my life who showed by example the meaning of public service and afforded me an opportunity for growth and development. I am forever in their debt.

Introduction

My name is Bill Robé. I am approaching my seventy-seventh birthday and will soon be going the way of the dinosaur. Before one moves on, and while the clock is still ticking, there comes a time to share the experiences of a full and rich life. Satisfaction comes from serving God, family, country, and humankind. As one who believes in God, has raised three children, and served his country both in the military and as a career federal civil servant, I cannot help but feel blessed.

As a young sailor who visited many parts of the world and was stationed for two years in a foreign land, I came to the conclusion that "there is no place like home." To witness poverty is to gain appreciation for the abundance we enjoy as Americans. To witness firsthand what most see only in the pictures in *National Geographic* magazine is to appreciate our American infrastructure. If only my fellow citizens could experience the sights, sounds, and smells of so many third-world countries, perhaps they would count their blessings rather than complain about our government and taxes. We must be doing something right and we are capable of doing even better.

As a career federal civil servant, working through the ranks (from GS-2 file clerk to GM-15 regional director), and living in numerous states, to become an executive within our federal government has indeed been rewarding. Witnessing life in ghettos and barrios has been an eye-opener. Experiencing the differences between people living in various parts of this great country has been an education in itself. Experience is worth a great deal—it promotes knowledge and understanding.

Taking numerous academic courses in a variety of accounting disciplines such as auditing, appraisals, statistics, and actuarial evaluations has given me cause to question many traditional and assumptive economic beliefs. In part 2, the *Domestic Spending Cycle* is explained in detail. This unique approach of tracking expenditures will intrigue readers. It will show conclusively that our national deficit should not and will not be controlled by lowering taxes and reducing all forms of government spending.

Readers concerned about high unemployment figures may be interested in the many doable and practical proposals outlined in parts 2 and 3.

I have written this book mainly to share my concerns over the future of our great country. Recent developments indicate that our form of government could collapse if we do not take remedial action. Yes, our democracy could go the way of past republics and cease to exist. What makes this even more regrettable is the fact that this collapse will be caused by internal strife and not by any invading army.

So many citizens are misguided in their understanding of democracy and our form of government. Many are beguiled by eloquent speeches given by those seeking elective office. Reading, understanding, and applying the concepts contained within this book could solve that problem. I truly hope so, for that is my intent!

This book should not be read like a novel. A quick read is meaningless. One must read each part and chapter, giving a measure of analytical thought to each subject. In so doing, the many dots presented in this book can be connected. A big picture will begin to formulate. Soon, the reader will visualize a clear and unobstructed view of the future—a future in which our form of government continues to prosper. Failure on the part of our citizens to connect the dots will lead to the end of our democracy. It becomes simply a matter of time before we will destroy ourselves. The Tea Party movement and the marches on Wall Street are but the beginnings of civil unrest. The polarization of political parties is a root cause.

Not everyone is aware of some of these basic concepts outlined in this book, so please bear with the author and give the less-informed a chance to catch up to your level of understanding if that is the case.

Please forgive the repetitive use of certain words and phrases such as "we the people," "common good," "freedom," and "unity." The repetition of these words and phrases is an attempt to drive home their importance. To gloss over them would do our form of government a great injustice.

Many citizens refer to federal executives as bureaucrats. Another goal in writing this book is to dispel such negative thinking by giving insight into the actions of government officials. Part 4 is my testimony before the US House of Representatives' Select Committee on Aging, which was held in Missoula, Montana, on April 17, 1983. It illustrates how executives within the government must sometimes act in order to preserve and protect the laws established by Congress.

The original demographics of our country have changed and will continue to change. This book takes into consideration those factual changes—for there is no going back to 1776. The conclusions reached in this book are based on the dynamics of demographic realism and not wishful thinking.

This book contains many ideas that will improve life amid ever-changing dynamics. If you enjoy your freedom and wish to experience a higher level of prosperity, you should adhere to the principles expressed in part 3. If you prefer to curse the darkness, then stay the present course and run the risk of losing your freedom. To maintain freedom and preserve our form of government requires effort and sacrifice. Is it worth it? Are we up to the challenge? We shall see—as we read on!

Pledge of Allegiance

I pledge allegiance to
the flag of the United States
of America,
and to the republic for which it stands,
one nation under God,
indivisible, with liberty and
justice for all.

We stand at attention, facing the flag, with our right hand over our heart, reaffirming the commitment of our Founding Fathers in 1776. The words expressed in this pledge are interwoven throughout the pages of this book. These words represent solidarity and unity of purpose for all people living within the framework of freedom through law.

PART 1

The Cause for Government

The Quest for Freedom

(What All People Hold in Common)

Oh, to be free! Free from duty. Free from responsibility. Free from the trials and tribulations caused by others. Free from rules, regulations, and laws. Unrestricted freedom—to come and go at will. To do what we want, when we want. To be subjected to no other human being. What a glorious dream! If one could only find such a life. One would have to be classified as a hermit, a leper, a loner, a social misfit, or perhaps a mountaintop guru or desert Bedouin in order to achieve such a high degree of freedom. The main question is: Can anyone live amid others and be totally free? Or is absolute freedom a myth—an internal siren song beckoning us to be individuals when in fact we are part of something larger than ourselves?

In holy matrimony the concept of two human beings uniting to become one might suggest that such an ideal situation is possible. In a symbolic gesture, the bride and the groom each hold a lighted candle. They go up to the altar and together light a larger candle representing their union. They then extinguish their individual candles, thus signifying that they are no longer individuals but are one in God's eyes. They are united. What a lovely thought. What a beautiful metaphor. It is little wonder that we cry at weddings!

Even in the best of marriages, the success of this concept depends on the couple's ability to give and to take. Each must be willing to give a little in order to strengthen the union. To do otherwise is to invite a strain in their relationship. They give up a portion of their freedom through love and not because of a law. Their loving partnership could weaken and will eventually become something less than a perfect union if one is always the giver, and the other is always the taker. Resentment has an ugly way of entering a once beautiful relationship.

When larger groups of unrelated humans come together to form a society, individual freedom must be sacrificed to a much greater degree in order for the various members to coexist in peace and harmony. During our Colonial and Revolutionary periods—back when people enjoyed more space and were not stepping on each others' toes as much—the need for rules, regulations, and restrictions was minimal. We must remember that the members of each colony held many moral and social views in common. The more we have in common, the safer we feel because of mutual understandings. Locks on doors and windows are less necessary. A simple handshake seals a business transaction. Jeffersonian thinking about small government was right for that time period, but alas, things have changed. (Our society is no longer a homogenous group of colonies but rather a blending of people from all over the world. What worked so well in 1776 has to be modified in order to keep up with those changes in our society.)

In their quest for freedom, the early settlers on the American continent tired of "taxation without representation" and rebelled. They wanted freedom from the English government—not freedom to run amuck. They wanted a government that was not oppressive and afforded personal freedom consistent with maintaining social order. Their craving has become our craving. As a result of the Revolutionary War, freedom is our heritage! It is now our birthright!

As we transformed from a rural to a more urban society, law and order with its many rules, regulations, and restrictions became increasingly necessary. This could be interpreted by many as a decline in individual freedom. The give-and-take associated with love and mutual respect must give way to obeying laws designed to maintain social order.

Part of belonging to a modern civilized society requires the ability to live in harmony with other human beings. We must allow others to seek their measure of freedom as long as they allow us that same consideration. It is once again a matter of give-and-take. It is being reasonable. It is being slow to anger and quick to forgive—or at least tolerate—the actions of others. This places restrictions and responsibilities on all of us as citizens and members of a society. Absolute freedom is a craving that can never be entirely satisfied if one is to live with others.

If we cannot have absolute freedom, then let us seek the maximum amount of freedom possible. The only way maximum freedom can prevail is through obedience to law. All laws should be enacted for the betterment of the common good. They must be fair, and they must be enforced; otherwise they are meaningless. A free society thus becomes a law-and-order society. Anything less will not guarantee a maximum amount of personal freedom. Toward this goal our government was established. As our population grows, the number of rules and regulations will, out of necessity, increase. A law-and-order government thus becomes the referee in the game of life so that one man's freedom does not become another man's enslavement. This is the essence of a democracy.

The vast majority of all restrictive laws, rules, and regulations stems from local governments via ordinances, permits, licenses, and similar restrictions. These local laws affect our daily lives much more than federal laws do. You will never find a federal marshal or an FBI agent handing out speeding tickets. Nevertheless, we lump all complaints about government together as if they stem from some form of Big Brother government. If a person wishes to be less restricted by government, he or she should move away from all towns or incorporated areas. Remember—the more the hermit, the greater degree of freedom! The larger the society, the more restrictions are required in order to coexist.

The word *freedom* means different things to different people. Some might consider themselves free if they are not in jail or a slave in bondage. For many others freedom is defined as having the ability to make choices. If there is no choice, then having the freedom to act is pointless. When there is a choice, then liberty/freedom can be exercised by selecting a course of action. Such actions can be considered either good or bad, depending on a given point of view.

It has been stated that a price must be paid for any measure of freedom. The maximum price would be the shedding of blood in order to fend off those who might attack our basic freedoms. To a lesser degree, we pay a price whenever we are forced to compromise our desires and demands. We can't always "have our cake and eat it too." We too will win some, and we will lose some. Such is the nature of a democracy. This is where politics and diplomacy enter the picture. At the end of each compromise, we should come away with the feeling that democracy was well served. There must be willingness on the part of those who did not get their way to observe the new, if less-desirable, rule or regulation. According to our Constitution—laws, rules, and regulations can be changed. In a democracy we must never give up hope for a better tomorrow.

Various radical groups demand liberty/freedom for themselves but are quick to limit the rights of others. For them, laws, rules, and regulations seem to be designed to keep others in check. During our frontier period, the law of the six-gun ruled—it settled many arguments.

The fastest and most accurate gunslinger won all disputes. Freedom reigned for those gunslingers, but everyone else became subservient to the "top gun." This is not what democracy is all about. Might does not always make right. Even a majority group cannot be allowed to prevail in its quest to dominate minorities in a democracy. If one believes his or her opinions are always right and other opinions are always wrong, one needs to look up the definition of bigotry.

As stated previously, a free society is a law-and-order society. Law and order give society a sense of security that shapes the destiny of a nation. We learn the limits of our desires and behave accordingly. We are mindful of the rights of others. We wish to live in peace and harmony. All laws, rules, and regulations are enacted by those elected by the people. This is referred to as representative government. We empower those elected representatives to do our bidding to the highest degree possible. They are our advocates, our voice, as they argue and debate our cause before their peers. The laws, rules, and regulations they enact should represent the common good and well-being of the people. Once a law, rule, or regulation is enacted, it should be obeyed; otherwise there is little point in having it on the books. Any law, rule, or regulation can be challenged through our judicial system. Every effort should be made to ensure that no legal actions detract from our rights as a free people. Failure to comply with a law could deprive a person of physical freedom resulting in jail time.

The Bill of Rights (the first ten Amendments to our Constitution) outlines our basic freedoms. Many societies in the world wish they could enjoy such guarantees. Does our government try to ensure that all citizens enjoy those same basic rights? Is our government depriving you of any rights? How do you feel about your personal freedom? Are you free enough?

When government enforces the laws placed on the books by officials elected by the people, is that an indication of a sinister "Big Brother Government"? Or is it a case of "we the people" attempting to live in harmony by securing a maximum amount of individual freedom?

In summarizing these comments on freedom, I have attempted to cover the following points:

1. There are many views regarding the nature and meaning of freedom.

2. Absolute freedom is impossible to find within a large society.

3. The larger the community, the more personal freedoms are restricted.

4. Law and order are required to maintain an agreed upon amount of freedom.

5. Government is needed to provide the required law and order.

One hopes that everyone is in agreement regarding personal freedom and is fully committed to guaranteeing others their rightful share. It was the cause that united our Founding Fathers. Now it is time to move on and discuss the importance of:

Individualism versus Unity

True individualism sometimes appears to be in opposition to total unity. In America we take great pride in declaring our individualism as a free people. In truth we are free only if we remain within the boundaries of our law-and-order society. We applaud creativity and ingenuity, while associating these qualities with those who might be considered geniuses.

We often admire the actions of a maverick or of those who think "outside the box." These feelings are but the reflections of one side of a coin. Often a maverick is nothing more than a loose cannon, a cowboy, or a nutcase. It is sometimes difficult to distinguish an undisciplined child from people in these categories. Such people can destroy unity and create chaos—while teams, choirs, and orchestras working in harmony can produce beautiful music. As citizens of a great nation, we should appreciate both creative individualism and the benefits of unity—developing the best of each in our quest for a more perfect union.

Individualism can be expressed in numerous ways without having an adverse effect on unity. People can dress differently or use makeup and hair dye to express individualism. They can surround themselves with articles that reflect their personality. They can decorate their homes and purchase unique automobiles for similar reasons. There are many ways to stand out in a crowd without being an eyesore! It is possible to belong to a group and still be an individual. We applaud individualism, which can be both creative and constructive. We should ignore the negative, self-centered, and greedy side of individualism.

As for the importance of unity—consider the following thoughts:
The quest for freedom was the driving force behind the Declaration of Independence. The colonists desired to govern themselves rather than be subjects of a British monarch. All thirteen colonies realized that

individually they could not overcome the might of the English army. They had to present a united front, acting as one if they were to have any chance of winning their independence. They named their new country the United States of America to show their solidarity. They knew the British army would be severely weakened if spread out along the entire Eastern seaboard of the North American continent.

Thus unity became the next major order of business in formulating a new government. This was a formidable task in that not all colonies had the same goals regarding freedom.

Southern states with large plantations demanded that slavery be allowed to continue, while the northern states felt that the practice of slavery was contrary to individual freedom and liberty. Had either side held rigidly to its beliefs, there would not have been a united front, and there might not have been a United States of America. It appears they reached a statesmanlike compromise that supported the wording of those early historical documents. One of the early acts of Congress was to pass a law that forbade the importation of new slaves into any state, with the hope that slavery would die a natural death over time. That idealistic dream was put to rest some four score and seven years later.

The importance of unity in our form of government cannot be overstated. "United we stand, divided we fall!" Abraham Lincoln understood that concept better than most men, since, in its breach, it led to the bloodiest of all wars (our Civil War). If an individual state or group of states could secede from the union for any reason, then our nation would soon unravel and collapse. Remembering the words in our Pledge of Allegiance ("one nation … indivisible") is a reflection of our desire to remain unified! Lincoln, by signing the Emancipation Proclamation, made the words in our Declaration of Independence more meaningful and our Constitution, with its Amendments, less hypocritical.

Unity supports the concepts of strength and security. To maintain our current status as a superpower, we must remain united. The former Soviet *Union* was considered a superpower before its threads of unity began to unravel. When other countries become smaller, we actually become more powerful. Their fragmentation and disunity make them less of a threat to our way of life. Would we feel more secure if Tibet, Xinjiang, Inner Mongolia, and the subdivisions of Manchuria broke away from China proper? Let us pray that they might squabble while we became more united in our ideals!

Unity means strength. Divisions are divisive! Setting nationalism aside for a moment, would the world be better off if all countries were united? Are there aspects of the United Nations that benefit all humankind while perhaps having a negative impact on individual countries? We will never enjoy peace on earth without countries becoming united in those basic principles outlined in our amended Constitution. Peace on earth will not occur during the foreseeable future, as we are a long way from having a united planet.

There are examples throughout the world (including the animal kingdom and "lower" forms of life) that show how unity brings about positive results. Working together for a common goal can lead to success. Disharmony results in failure and lack of achievement. When we tear each other apart through such actions as name-calling and lies, we are picking away at the threads of harmony and unity. We can thus become our own worst enemy. These are the seeds that have caused other great civilizations to fail—these would be the reaping of the enemy within. (Let us reflect on our present situation for a moment.)

A lone human has difficulty accomplishing major undertakings, but united with others who have the same goals and aspirations, he or she can achieve much. The history of the Amish, the Mennonites, the Mormons, and other groups, who work together in love and fellowship, provides examples of successful unification overcoming great obstacles.

One need only observe a beehive, an ant colony, or a wolf pack to see examples of how other creatures have learned to work together for a common goal. World War II united our country to such a degree that we even surprised ourselves. We were caught up in a common goal to defeat an enemy on two fronts. We excelled, and virtually overnight we went from a sleepy agricultural nation to become a world power. We need to revisit that spirit of unity once again. Unity begot our freedom, and unity continues to maintain our freedom!

What keeps us from being a more united country? Why did the Founding Fathers use the opening phrase in our Constitution—"We the People of the United States, *in Order to form a more perfect Union* [emphasis added], establish Justice ..."? What is meant by the words "a more perfect Union"? Surely we all desire a perfect union—so why did they say a more perfect union? Did they realize that humans are not perfect and can never be perfect? Can we strive for a more perfect union but never achieve it, no matter how hard we try? It would appear that our Founding Fathers understood the complexities of the human spirit and chose those words carefully.

While searching for unattainable perfection within our society, we must make allowances for the weaknesses within the human race. The reasons for disharmony are numerous. We are not clones but creatures with individual qualities, talents, and characteristics. Our IQ levels vary (from those of the mentally deficient to those of a genius), with many ratings considered within the range of normalcy. Some of us have physical disabilities that complicate our lives and hamper our productivity. Some of us are simply insane! The cause matters not—the fact is, we are different, our opinions are different, and our approach to problem-solving is different. There are more than three hundred million people in our country, with almost as many opinions on any given subject. We could achieve much greater goals if we all heard the beat of the same drummer.

There has never been a law passed that has been found to be absolutely perfect. Every law—even our beloved Constitution—has been amended time after time. Each Amendment represents a desired improvement or perhaps the plugging of a loophole. Make any law, no matter how beneficial, and someone will find a way to circumvent the intent of that law. The author offers his 2 percent theory. Make a law that is 98 percent perfect, and one could say it is "good enough for government work." (A 98 percent grade in school would earn an A+!) Never expect perfection in any of man's endeavors, and you will never be totally disappointed.

There are many who support the basic concept of unity but are quick to condemn unionism. Many strongly support individualism while at the same time reaping the benefits of standardization and uniformity. Inconsistency in thinking is a human failing.

Here is one example of such an inconsistency: When shopping, many citizens find it helpful to read the now required labeling concerning the packaging and contents of edible products. Perhaps they have a special dietary need or concern such as the restrictions associated with diabetes. The labels are on these products because of government regulations and oversight; they are not the product of any benevolent producer within the private sector. Many citizens enjoy these labeling requirements yet demand smaller government.

Rural citizens enjoy more fresh foods, while those living in the cities must rely heavily on processed foods. Such processed foods could be without nutritional value or contain harmful ingredients. Wouldn't the city dwellers like to know what they are eating?

There are numerous situations involving government intervention or oversight that enhance our standard of living. In the past, how many parents even thought about lead in their children's toys? Building codes and other government requirements have proven their worth during times of earthquakes. Need we be thankful for government rules and regulations? Do we wish to go back to "the good old days" when food processors, building contractors, and other manufacturers were left to their own devices?

Government rules and regulations have given us safer cars, baby car seats, helmets, and a list of other products that goes on and on—all in the name of the common good.

Oftentimes standardization will speed up our selection process, thus affording more time for other endeavors. When making plumbing repairs, isn't it nice to have certain standards regarding pipe size, threads, and fittings? Think about those manufacturing notices on electrical products. Standardization can be found in many segments of retailing, manufacturing, and construction applications. While creativity (individualism) is a wonderful thing, the assembly line (uniformity and standardization) makes it possible for more people to enjoy that which has been created. The government has been involved in standardization in many areas of our lives. Are you comfortable shopping for "Buyer Beware" products? What is the real value of the Consumer Protection Agency?

When speaking of unity, we must speak in unity. Our national language is English. If we are to be one nation, then we must speak one language. In the Old Testament (Genesis 11:5–8) there is the story about the Tower of Babel. The confounding of tongues caused the people to scatter—no longer united. When the Jewish people established their country back in the late 1940s, Jews gathered from all parts of the world, each speaking the language of the foreign country from which they came. In order to build their new nation, they spoke the common language of their religion (Hebrew). The ability to speak and understand one another was vital to the establishment of their new state. This point is no less important today in America as it was for the previously scattered Jewish people.

Allow me to interject a personal story. My father was born a second generation German American. He grew up in the German ghetto on Chicago's near north side. In school he and his siblings were taught in both English and German. He married a girl who came from an English colonial heritage. When his children were born, he firmly insisted that his siblings not teach his children to speak German. He would often state: "They are Americans—not Germans."

I am truly sorry I never learned to speak German as a second language, but I can appreciate his rationale. We are Americans! All newly arrived citizens would do well to develop my father's patriotism—making certain their children become well-adjusted members of our society as quickly as possible. By keeping various heritages alive we enrich our society and expand our menus in order that we might now enjoy, pizza, chow mein, Irish stew, borscht, and similar traditional foreign foods.

There is nothing we could not achieve as a nation if we remain united. Let us shun those who would tear us apart. Many will claim to be patriots and wrap themselves in our flag while attempting to destroy those who disagree with their philosophy; yet they offer little in return. Let us return to the true meaning of the phrase: "Good enough for government work." It was not meant as a slur but rather a standard of high quality. We need checks and balances in all of life, not only in government. Some people will make or do anything for a quick buck—setting standards lessens the negative effects of such individuals. Let us be united in a quest for high quality—for the makers of inferior products (like the poor) will always be with us.

Working together for the common good draws us nearer to a more perfect union. Hermits and loners will never understand the concept of unity. For the reader who understands that freedom and unity make our country a superpower, read on. For the reader who cannot understand these principles, close the book, as it will serve no useful purpose for you.

In summarizing this segment, I hope the reader will understand the following points:

1. A limited number of individuals are truly creative and capable of benefiting society because of their ingenuity.

2. To stifle their activities and contributions would be counterproductive to the needs of our society.

3. Aside from those truly gifted individuals, most citizens would better serve the needs of our country by uniting with their peers in order to promote the common good.

4. Unity of the masses represents strength and security for the nation.

5. Unity overcomes disagreements and promotes achievement.

6. Uniformity, coupled to standardizations, increases and improves productivity.

7. Government plays an important role in setting standards that benefit society as a whole.

8. A common tongue strengthens the concept of unity.

9. It is unity that promotes our liberty, not individualism. (*One nation* under God, *indivisible*, with liberty and justice for *all* [emphasis added].)

Our Form of Government

Seeking freedom through unity led our Founding Fathers to the next order of business. What form of government did they desire for their new nation? They were not looking for a king or a dictator to replace the English monarch. They wanted a government run by the people as in a republic, yet they wanted even more. They wanted a republic where all citizens were equal in rank and in privileges—they wanted a democracy.

The wording in our Constitution qualifies our country as a republic. The Bill of Rights upgrades and qualifies our republic as a democracy. As good Americans we should have a clear understanding as to our exact form of government. The United States of America is a *democratic republic*. There are many forms of democracies, and there are many forms of republics in the world today.

Our government represents an excellent blend of both terms. Both forms (democracies and republics) apply to governments that are controlled by the people they govern. The Constitution begins with the words "We the people."

In more recent years, the meaning of the word *republic* has become somewhat distorted. Once upon a time there was a government called the Union of Soviet Socialist *Republics* (USSR or the Soviet Union); that country claimed to be a union of *republics*. Today there are countries such as the People's *Republic* of China and the Democratic People's *Republic* of North Korea, neither of which could be properly compared to our form of a republic.

In reciting the Pledge of Allegiance, we state, "to the Republic *for which it stands*" (emphasis added), and this indicates that our republic stands for something. In short, our Republic stands for democracy! Our interpretation of a republic does not exist in communistic forms of republican governments. Nor do all our freedoms, as outlined in the Bill of Rights, exist within the framework of other democracies. We are special—the most blessed nation on Earth—because of this blending of principles.

One might well ask, "What is the difference between those two words if both represent a government of the people?" In a republic there is an allowance for a class system (for example, any social pecking order such as "free" or "slave") *and* the belief that majority rules in all elections. In a democracy, a class system should not exist and, while the majority rules in most situations, the majority is not allowed to subvert the rights of the minority. In short—the majority cannot suppress a minority. The majority cannot enact laws that trample on the rights of the minority. In a democracy, everyone must be treated equally under the law.

Many of our present-day citizens think more like Republicans while others think more like Democrats—and this is not meant in the political party sense. Republican-minded individuals are strongly in favor of majority rule and can easily adapt to living within a class system. Democrats stress equality among people.

Without the first ten Amendments to the Constitution, slavery would still be allowed, and any minority group could be disenfranchised. The might of any majority could override the rights of any minority. Thus might, would make right in all situations. Heaven help those who are not members of a majority movement—be it a religion, political party, or ethnic group. Did our Founding Fathers make the correct choice by adding the Bill of Rights to our Constitution? (Without it, we would be just another France with a different organizational chart.)

This is a perfect place to stop and assess your personal value system. Can you see the divide that is taking place within our country? You are free to make a choice. You can vote for the extreme right-wing view or the extreme left-wing view. A person can be a moderate on many minor issues, but when push comes to shove on any important issue, which way will you go? In part 2 we will be discussing the important issues of the day. At the end of each issue, ask yourself: "Am I a Republican thinker or am I a Democratic thinker?" Once again, do not ask that question as a member of a political party. Ask it as an independent thinker, and be honest with your feelings.

In a good democracy the strong are required to protect the rights of the weak. There are some famous words inscribed on the walls at Boys Town, near Omaha, Nebraska, which simply state, "He ain't heavy, Father; he's my brother!" Perhaps such words should be considered food for thought in a caring democratic nation.

The main framework of the Constitution sets up the structure of our government. It contains required information regarding the three branches of government—executive, legislative, and judicial. Many might consider the Constitution an organizational chart. Much of the appeal for this document exists in the "checks and balances" found therein. It keeps the individual branches from dominating one another. For anything worthwhile to be achieved, there must be a measure of unity involved.

After determining the type of government we were to have, the next order of business involved determining how government should be run. Some wanted the federal government to have the larger voice in determining the affairs of the states. Others wanted a smaller federal government, with each state having the larger voice in governing the citizens of that state.

The thirteen colonies took great pride in their individual identities. The majority of the colonies had been established with differing religious beliefs, customs, and traditions. They were easily drawn to the idea of each state being a sovereign entity within this new nation. A popular opinion of that era was for each state to be autonomous.

In order to accommodate two levels of government (federal and state), each state has its own constitution. The only limitation is that no state constitution can override the authority and freedoms granted in the federal Constitution. This is an indication that federalism was intended to be the dominate form of government. It is this federation that makes us a nation.

The various state constitutions (now fifty in number) tend to have many of the same features as the federal Constitution, yet several differences can be found when comparing these documents. A few state constitutions have been amended because of federal Supreme Court rulings over the years. Each individual state enjoys having its own State Supreme Court. The names for lower courts may vary from state to state, yet the overall legal framework remains similar to that of the federal system. Most states have two legislative bodies (an upper and a lower house), yet there are exceptions to these arrangements in certain states. In short, both systems can work together in harmony, which adds meaning to our national motto: *"e pluribus unum"* (out of many, one).

A faction within the Continental Congress believed that the superior level of government should be the federal or centralized government. This group included such great Founding Fathers as George Washington, John Adams, Alexander Hamilton, and John Jay (the first chief justice of the Supreme Court). These gentlemen and others who agreed with them were part of the Federalist movement.

The Federalist Papers of that era are a testament to their many differences of opinion as to how best to run the new republic. (*The Federalist Papers* consisted of eighty-five articles published during the first twenty-five years of our republic. Hamilton wrote fifty-one of those articles; James Madison, our fourth president, wrote twenty-nine; and John Jay wrote five.) Many Federalists agreed with Thomas Jefferson, who championed individual freedom and thereby made it easier for James Madison and others to switch, later on, from the Federalist movement to Jefferson's Democratic-Republican Party.

We must remember that George Washington was not the commanding general of any one state or colony; rather, he was the general of the entire Continental Army. Most citizens within the thirteen colonies knew their beloved and victorious general. His popularity and name recognition made him the obvious choice to be the first popularly elected president. His vice president, John Adams, likewise felt that the federal government was best suited to govern the new nation. Both men held a broad view regarding the importance of unity.

George Washington created the first four cabinet positions to help him run the new country. He appointed Thomas Jefferson as the first Secretary of State. Alexander Hamilton, who believed strongly in a central banking system, became the first Secretary of the Treasury. Henry Knox became the first Secretary of War (now known as the Secretary of Defense), and Edmund Randolph became the first US Attorney General. The Federalist movement lasted fewer than twenty years before fading into the pages of history.

While in existence, the Federalists helped to bind the states into one nation. Washington's Secretary of the Treasury, Alexander Hamilton, was responsible for our having a federalized banking and economic system. Much more will be said about our economic system (capitalism) later in this book.

Toward the end of George Washington's administration, Thomas Jefferson began to express his feelings more aggressively. Jefferson, a prolific writer and statesman, argued that the people would be better served by local governments, rather than some far-off, centralized government. He argued extensively against big government. He reasoned that any government capable of giving you everything was capable of taking everything away. His rationale and reasoning won him a place in the White House as our third president and leader of the then newly formed Democratic-Republican Party.

Jefferson was one of the brightest statesmen of his time. Many of his writings and statements will go down in the history books for future generations to ponder. There appears to be a human side to this man. One finds a great deal of hypocrisy involving moral issues when one compares his writings with his personal actions. He wrote that all men were free and created equal—yet he owned many slaves. One of his female slaves bore him many children. When do slaves have the right to deny their master's wishes? How close would such actions be called rape or statutory rape in our modern-day society?

Jefferson, the anti–big government champion, was quick to make the Louisiana Purchase using money from the *federal* central bank. He obviously did not think of this as hypocritical. As a very wealthy and influential citizen within the state of Virginia, Jefferson preferred states' rights over the larger central government. Was he ensuring the long-term success of his magnificent Monticello manor? Because of his position in Virginia, he held much sway over the Virginia government in contrast to the uncertainties of dealing with the central government. His motives might not have been as pure as we have been led to believe. Some might conclude that he was feathering his own nest.

Four presidents—Thomas Jefferson, James Madison, James Monroe, and John Quincy Adams (1801 to 1829)—were members of the Democratic-Republican Party. Internal strife caused the extinction of that party in 1829. Andrew Jackson became president—the first president to bear the Democratic Party label. This split caused the Whig Party to emerge from the dying Democratic-Republican Party. The Antebellum Period (the time period prior to the Civil War) saw the presidency switching back and forth between the Democrats and the Whigs. The Whig Party fell into disarray, and a dark horse named

Abraham Lincoln emerged as president. He was the first to be called simply a Republican. This left us with the two current major political parties—Democrats and Republicans.

Since then, several individuals have attempted to form additional parties (such as the Bull Moose Party, the Libertarians, the Green Party, etc.), but to no avail. There are many individuals who do not wish to be affiliated with either of the major political parties, and they are referred to as Independents.

Those who tire of the two-party system believe there should be more parties. This might best be referred to as fragmentation of government. The more divided we become; the harder it is to reach consensus on a vote that does not reflect an absolute majority view. An absolute majority requires 51 percent in favor of either a person or a law. If an election is divided three ways, it is unlikely one person or law would receive a majority. It is true that one person or law would receive the most votes, but that person or law is weakened by not having the support of a majority. In many countries throughout the world, multiple parties are allowed, which often leads to the formation of a weakened coalition government. While the Constitution makes allowances for multiple parties, it would not appear to be in our best interest to encourage fragmentation.

Third parties are normally very weak in that they have a limited agenda. They lack the ability to run a country of our size. They may well be strong on a few domestic issues but usually lack any expertise in foreign or military affairs.

Those citizens who claim to be Independents can be divided into two major categories. There are those Independents who simply cannot find anything good to say about politicians. Then there are those who like certain aspects of both parties and prefer to vote with an independent mind. The latter make excellent citizens, while the naysayer simply loves to bitch and moan, having nothing worthwhile to offer.

Within the two major parties there is a wide range of ideals and opinions. Labels are used to indicate certain positions. Terms like conservative, liberal, and progressive are used. Then we have the extremist wings in both parties, with the middle-of-the-road people somewhere in between. Let us not forget the "hawks" versus the "doves." We have plain old conservatives, fiscal conservatives, and social conservatives. This labeling goes on and on, and it isn't long before you realize there are no two people alike in either party. People band together for basic ideological beliefs and end up disliking those who disagree with their point of view.

There is only one thing for certain—the two-party system is better than a one-party system. In order for humanity to stay on the straight and narrow, there must be opposition in all things. Over time, any group with too much power will generally attempt to dominate the other groups. Unfortunately, in more recent times the parties have become so set in their ways that they can no longer achieve consensus. Party has become more important than the common good. One-upmanship has become a way of life in the political arena. For all of our sakes, this behavior must come to an end.

Perhaps there is no easy solution to this dilemma. Back in 1776 the representatives of each colony sat next to one another. They represented their colony or state. They worked together for the common good of their respective colonies. Then, those colonies with similar problems and ideology sat together for support and the sharing of ideas. Today, both houses of Congress have installed an invisible barrier called the aisle. Democrats sit on one side and the Republicans on the other. Each state has two senators. If the state has senators of different parties, there is a tendency to vote along party lines, which cannot serve the best interests of their supporters back home. They are canceling out each other's votes. We have divided our country into "blue" states and "red" states. Would it not be better for all of us if they became "red, white, and blue" states?

In reviewing this segment we have discussed these issues:

1. We are a unique country, being both a republic and a true democracy.

2. The actual document we refer to as the Constitution establishes the fact that our form of government is a republic. It is the Bill of Rights—the first ten Amendments to that Constitution—that makes our country a democracy.

3. The importance of the individual states over the federal government was unquestionably the majority opinion of our countrymen during the early days of our republic. A rural society has less need for government rules and regulations. A large civil urban society cannot exist without them.

This past segment was more of an historical overview of early events. While the political parties were changing, so was the country. It was growing in size both in population as well as territory. The railroads would link our two oceans. The Native Americans lost their right to roam the land. The buffalo almost became extinct. Yes, change was in the air! These changes are challenging us to amend our thinking. There is no retreating—let us now examine some events that will highlight the evolutionary aspects of our society.

Changing Demographics

Westward expansionism opened up a seemingly endless frontier for growth, individualism, and opportunity. Horses and oxen-pulled wagons preceded the laying of tracks for the railroads. Stampedes of people occurred as they laid claim for homesteading on the new frontier. The US Department of the Interior was established in 1849 to address the needs of this exploding expansionism. Law and order sometimes had a difficult time keeping up with this westward migration and lawlessness ran rampant in many towns for several decades. Little thought was given to the government back in Washington, DC, but for the military, which afforded some protection against hostile natives.

The American frontier was known throughout Europe for its cowboys and Indians. The law of the six-gun predated the judicial system. The early settlers were of hardy stock—independent, resourceful, and virtually fearless. They handled problems without needing government involvement. They were truly free spirits—if you exclude all the things they *had* to do in order to survive.

The majority of those early settlers were farmers scratching their living out of the soil. So agriculture was the No. 1 method of survival for those early settlers. In 1889 the US Department of Agriculture was established to address the needs of farmers.

Toward the end of the 1800s, the majority of our rich and wealthy citizens lived east of the Appalachian Mountains with a few groups living in the more metropolitan areas of St. Louis and Chicago. This nucleus formed a grouping of four hundred rich families, who became known in 1920 as "high society." The young daughters of the rich were known as debutantes and given lavish coming-of-age parties by their parents. Their children were sent to Ivy League universities where the children joined fraternities and sororities in order to develop social networks befitting their class. An economic class system was developing. Many of those within this upper class began to find ways of being even more affluent than others. The seeds of greed were being planted in this developing class system's fertile soil.

The rich had to find ways of becoming richer, so the nation witnessed the development of sweatshops, exploiting women and children, cutting corners to produce a more lucrative bottom line. To counteract this development, organized labor unions were being formed in several major cities. Many union leaders wished to share in the prosperity of the rich, while others were more concerned with health and safety issues. Around 1913 two new government departments—the US Department of Commerce and the US Department of Labor—were formed to address the growing concerns of both business and labor. The United States was rapidly embracing the spirit of the Industrial Revolution— lagging more than a century behind Europe.

As an emerging industrial nation, we became ripe for war. In 1916 we were sucked into just another one of many European wars. The United States, along with the various member countries of the British Empire, turned a run-of-the-mill European war into a World War. Nearly 117,000 US servicemen lost their lives during this conflict.

Many of our young farm boys—now men who had experienced the horrors of war—returned home and could not find employment. The lyrics from a popular song of the time were "How're you gonna keep 'em down on the farm after they have seen Paree [Paris]?" The government was not keeping up with promised benefits to veterans, and this eventually led to organized veteran marches on Washington, DC. The president ordered US Army General Douglas MacArthur to break up those demonstrations. This placed the regular army in the position of denying former comrades the right to assemble. A future president (Ike) learned a great deal from this unpleasant situation.

The eighteenth Amendment (Prohibition) to the Constitution became law in 1919. This was followed a year later by the nineteenth Amendment giving women the right to vote. Both ushered in the infamous Roaring Twenties. The mobster element surfaced to wreak havoc in our major cities. We were slowly becoming an urban nation as more people were living in large towns and cities rather than on farms. The need for law and order became more acute.

Can the reader visualize the metamorphosis that had taken place over the years? We remained a nation of small farmers during the formative years. The westward expansion was so rapid that law and order had a hard time keeping up with it. We were a nation of free individuals having little need for any form of government. That bygone society has gone bye-bye! We can never go back in time to the rugged, gun-toting days of the cowboy, for we will not give up our indoor plumbing! (We had *theoretically* become a more civilized society.)

Modern-day politicians proclaim their desire to return the nation to the principles set forth by the Founding Fathers. They claim we are losing our liberty, freedom, and individualism as set forth in the founding documents. They are using appealing rhetorical words to win votes. They are not dealing with reality. Beware of good-sounding words that are hollow in application. Many politicians tug at the strings of our heart but are unable to deliver solutions. We must ask them point blank to describe the legal course of action they would take to achieve their desired goal. Be on the lookout for evasive answers.

Without a doubt, we would all enjoy having more liberty and freedom. What sane person wouldn't? But we have a way of forgetting the negative aspects of those "good old days." We must set our sights on the future, for there is no way we can go back. We cannot pick and choose events from the past without affecting all the other events that have taken place. Modern people are not ready or willing to dwell in caves in order to achieve maximum freedom. If we wish to move forward, we must stop sounding retreat!

So—sound the charge! Let us make further advances and reap the rewards of progress.

The Great Depression

It is extremely important to point out at this time that, from the presidency of Abraham Lincoln (1861) until the inauguration of Franklin D. Roosevelt (1933), there were thirteen Republican presidents and only two Democratic presidents. Fifty-six republican years versus sixteen democratic years is a strong indication of the ideological tendencies of the nation. This is evidence of a strong belief in small, unobtrusive government, which prevailed during that entire period. There were no checks and balances outside of government. Government was told to mind its own business. Our economic engine (capitalism) was developing slowly by trial and error during this period.

During the first 155 years of our country, Adam Smith's capitalism, warts and all, reigned supreme! No one was watching the developing symptoms of greed taking place within commerce! No checks—no balances! No oversight had made us myopic! We were operating in the dark. The Great Depression of 1929 was on its way, and no one saw it coming!

As we look for a cause of the stock market crash leading up to the Great Depression, can the blame be laid at the doorstep of family farmers, ranchers, or small entrepreneurs? Could it have been caused by the housewives or blue- and white-collar workers living within the cities? Surely a financial crash of such magnitude had to start somewhere within the banking and investment sector of the economy. It was not the fault of the average individual citizen. Because the government was not involved to any degree with the affairs of business, there are no records to indicate who the actual guilty parties were. No government entity was holding the business sector accountable for its actions. Our "stay-out-of-the-affairs-of-business" government was not to blame, for it was merely following the wishes of the people. Capitalistic greed was allowed to run amuck without the necessary checks and balances, thus causing the Great Depression.

A chain of events occurred rapidly. The stock market crashed, panic filled the air, five thousand banks went out of business, investors lost their savings, and more panic and fear followed. No one, not even the president of the United States, was able to stem the tide. Homes and farms were lost to foreclosures, unemployment levels soared, and breadlines formed, as our capitalistic economic system failed. A dark cloud was gathering over a great agricultural nation.

President Hoover wrung his hands in despair. He hadn't the slightest clue as to how to go about solving this calamity. He tried to balance his budget, thinking that would help, but unfortunately that only made matters worse. Everyone was waiting for the natural attributes of capitalism somehow to come alive and save the day. Let us be perfectly clear on this point: had the government not become involved, the United States of America would not exist today. Anarchy would have prevailed. The masses, out of desperation, would have rebelled, thus putting an end to our wonderful form of government.

During the early 1930s there appeared upon the scene a member of the elite American upper class. He was born into a family that held a long tradition of conservative values. He was related to a former president, Teddy Roosevelt. He had come to the realization that the Jeffersonian ideology of a small, unobtrusive federal government was failing. What he was about to do turned many of his closest friends against him. He was going against his upper-class upbringing in favor of the middle-class and the poor.

In 1932, Franklin D. Roosevelt was elected president. During his campaign, he promised a modified economic plan that he referred to as the "New Deal." The main attributes of capitalism would remain intact while the federal government would become more involved in economic and social issues. Concerning the New Deal, one of his closest friends and adviser said to Roosevelt, "Franklin, if your plan works, you will go down in history as our greatest president." To which FDR replied, "Yes, but if I fail, I will be known as the last American president." The stakes were extremely high. The nation's ship of state was either headed for Davy Jones's locker or toward the uncharted horizon of the future. (This is a metaphoric expression indicating it was time to either scuttle our democratic form of government or set a new course into an uncertain future—a case of sink or swim!)

During his initial campaign he gave very few details as to how his plan would work. By keeping his plan vague until after his inauguration, he increased his chances for success. Critics love to criticize, especially when they have nothing better to offer! It is far easier to find fault with someone's plan than it is to find a solution to a problem.

Many people despised FDR—among them, none other than outgoing President Hoover. Hoover had no idea how the current economic situation could be altered. He knew the economy was headed downward, and society was spinning out of control, yet he thought FDR was little more than an opportunist.

A newsreel film showing the two of them leaving the White House for the inauguration ceremony pictures a depressed and solemn Hoover and a smiling, waving FDR. One president represented failure and defeat, the other hope and optimism. FDR deserved far more than name-calling and belittlement. He proved to be a man who answered his nation's call during a time of great need and, in so doing, served us well by saving our nation from extinction. In my opinion, this man must go down in history as one of our greatest presidents.

Having the federal government more involved in economic and social endeavors is not dissimilar to the position taken by the Federalists back in the late 1700s. Capitalism would still be capitalism under the New Deal, yet it would be modified by allowing government to be more involved in economic issues. As we have moved somewhat away from Adam Smith's theory, perhaps we should call our economic system "American capitalism." American capitalism has a heart, while no heart is required in uncontrolled, old-fashioned capitalism. It is heartless capitalism that often creates the image of "Ugly Americans" around the world.

The reader should not equate American capitalism with another form of government called socialism. In socialism, the government owns and operates business, while the workers share equally in the output of that business. In American capitalism, the government does not own or operate any business; free enterprise reigns supreme! The government merely directs traffic, keeping crashes to a minimum. (Keeping our eyes open and our headlights turned on will avoid many future accidents.)

Many forms of government (especially democracies) make allowance for social needs. Food stamps and unemployment benefits address social needs but need not be part of a socialist government. The reader should understand the differences when using these words. FDR was not attempting to replace capitalism with socialism.

FDR enacted many programs that he hoped would stimulate the economy. Several programs failed, but many more survived the test of time—having been declared constitutional by the US Supreme Court. We must remember that no large, private enterprise came to the rescue of the weakened economy. It was FDR who put people to work on the government payroll. Money in the hands of those workers, along with his constant reminder that "we have nothing to fear but fear itself," helped develop consumer confidence. Because of Roosevelt's actions, the economy was on the mend, and the country began to climb slowly out of the (depression) hole it had found itself in. "Happy Days Are Here Again" became an uplifting song during that era.

If the private sector is unable to get things rolling economically, the federal government would be well-advised to revisit the FDR era for an example of how to get the job done.

FDR's approach to the problems of his time indicates that he was a progressive thinker. Change of any type is hard for many people to handle. There is a certain amount of comfort in knowing the outcome, even in troublesome situations. Many individuals appear to like making the same mistakes over and over again because of the known outcome. Trying something new is risky and the outcome uncertain. Why else would certain individuals insist on reducing government employment to balance a budget and reduce the deficit, when in fact it is counterproductive to do so? Why else would these same individuals believe that reducing government oversight is going to lessen the monetary problems brought about by corporate greed? It would seem that they enjoy having a depression every twenty-five or thirty years. Why else? Anyone can make a mistake—once. It takes a village (full of idiots) to keep repeating the same mistake. To err is human—to forgive is a lapse of memory or an early sign of dementia!

As a result of FDR's efforts, "safety nets" were being provided for our people. Older Americans (at that time sixty-five years of age was considered old) had a tough time finding work and, for that matter, competing with younger workers who had families to feed. Various social issues found voice during his administration. Many began to call FDR a socialist and a communist. Nothing could have been further from the truth. Having compassion and a sense of responsibility for one's fellow human beings should not be mistaken for something sinister. This physically handicapped president was elected four times, despite his condition. His perseverance and dedication to his beliefs won him the hearts of most Americans.

FDR's cabinet grew in size during his administration because government was growing. More programs required more helpers to oversee so many new programs. The days of a small, unobtrusive government had come to an end. The genie had escaped from the bottle. There is no going back to the "good old days." As we come to this ideological juncture, should we continue to fight the tide of needed change or should we climb on board willingly and sail into a future of hope? Collectively, "we the people" can achieve greatness. All we have to do is learn to work together for the *common good*.

The Great Depression was an historical event. Much has been written on this subject. The reader will be able to find a great deal of reading material confirming this tragic event. This past segment should have revealed the following:

1. The cause of the Great Depression was a flaw in uncontrolled capitalism.

2. No private enterprise was capable of solving this nationwide crisis.

3. The federal government was the only entity capable of stemming the tide.

Winding Up the Past

Since the administration of FDR, we have had six Democrat and six Republican presidents—with more actual Republican years in office. Each president left his mark on the pages of history—some showing strengths and others weaknesses. Rather than trying to discuss all their characteristics, I would like to select those actions that reflect (positively or negatively) on the theme of this book.

As a veteran, my personal feeling is that the shedding of American blood on foreign soil, when it is not in direct defense of our homeland, is inexcusable. This would include all wars fought since World War II. We need only look at the final results of those conflicts to assess their value. Countless lives lost, thousands of bodies mutilated, our treasure greatly diminished, resulting in so little to show for all that suffering and loss. I honor all personal sacrifices made by our service personnel on behalf of our country. Lest anyone believe that I am a dove, be assured that I believe in using bombs, missiles, and air strikes when necessary. I am simply against putting American boots on someone else's ground. Nothing in our Constitution mandates that we become a world power. When was the last time some other country came to our rescue during one of our wars? Was it 1776, 1812, or 1861? Did they put large numbers of their boots on our ground, next to ours? Did they become our liberators or were those wars left up to us, either to win or to lose? We need at least to consider President Eisenhower's admonishment to "beware the military-industrial complex" before taking military action. Perhaps we could then determine why we are putting our collective noses into someone else's business. Could it be for someone's profit?

Many actions taken by the various former administrations have been excluded from the following comments. These comments are for illustrative purposes (relative to the contents of this book) only:

Under the Truman administration the United Nations was formed, and it should prove most beneficial to our overall democratic ideology as we become a more global society. The Korean conflict began, and sixty years later, nearly 30,000 troops remain in that country.

Under the Eisenhower administration the Interstate Highway System was built, and it proved to be a boon to our economy. By providing nationwide employment opportunities on a massive scale, many unskilled construction and transportation jobs were filled by returning Korean and WWII veterans in need of employment.

The next presidential election resulted in controversy. The Kennedy administration's emphasis on space exploration created thousands of technical jobs and paved the way for more research and technical advances. The Peace Corps was established. The Vietnam conflict began.

Under the (LBJ) Johnson administration, both the Civil Rights Act and the Medicare Act were signed into law. Democracy was advanced, and the health needs of our older citizens were addressed. The Vietnam conflict escalated into a full-scale war.

The Nixon administration brought much shame to the executive branch of government. The vice president, Spiro Agnew, was removed from office in disgrace. The resignation of the president soon followed. Cynicism over government escalated. Dirty tricks became an acceptable part of politics! The twenty-fifth Amendment to the Constitution ushered in a caretaker president named Gerald Ford, the only president not elected by the direct vote of the people.

During the Reagan administration, an official campaign to reduce government rules and regulations was put into effect. Many federal jobs were eliminated due to the efforts of Vice President George H. W. Bush. The negative results of these actions would take years to surface. Unemployment soared, and the annual deficit reached an all-time high for a nation not at war.

Under the Clinton administration, the computer age came to life within the federal government, creating more jobs, while lowering the deficit for only the second time in history. This was accomplished through the efforts of Vice President Gore. The personal shortcomings of the president made us less than proud of our president.

The George W. Bush administration began under a cloud. The election results were questionable. The Iraqi War was avoidable. The president looked into the eyes of a former Russian KGB director and saw his soul and concluded he was a good, honorable man. The results of an earlier administration's deregulation policy became evident when an economic meltdown began. Thousands of people lost their homes; unemployment reached its highest levels since the Great Depression. Banks and insurance companies failed in large numbers. The automobile industry was brought to its knees. Fears of another depression filled the air. It would appear that we have learned little since 1929 in terms of controlling capitalism. If we keep making the same mistakes over and over again, we can be assured that history will repeat itself.

Please note from the preceding discussion that both positive and negative points came from both sides of the political aisle. We must keep in mind that we want and need a two-party system. In terms of ideology, our nation is still divided in many ways. We must now realize that the past is behind us, and blame serves no useful purpose. Let us now face the problems past administrations caused, or left unaddressed, as we prepare for the future.

We have all heard the expression, "Figures don't lie, but liars figure." In government, this is sometimes referred to as using "smoke and mirrors" in order to impress the voters. I recall two amusing incidents during my years of service that I will now introduce to illustrate this point.

One candidate for the presidency (Eisenhower) campaigned on the promise that he would cut 50,000 government jobs if elected president. He won and felt compelled to keep his promise. His political hacks instructed all agencies of government to submit a list of currently vacant positions that were not vital to the mission of that agency. They then ordered the removal of those vacant positions from the official records. When the number 50,000 was reached, the administration announced that the president had kept his promise. Not one person was laid off, and not one dime was saved. The public was well-satisfied with their new president. He was a man of honor who kept his word!

During his term of office, sitting president Ronald Reagan became concerned over the growing number of unemployed. This was placing his administration in an unfavorable light. Something had to be done. Prior to this time, the military forces of our nation were not included as part of the national workforce. Of course there is no unemployment in the military. Adding this large block of fully employed people to the national workforce figure caused the official unemployment rate to be lowered by half a percentage point overnight. The public noted the decline and praised the president for his achievement.

Neither of these incidents caused harm to our country. This is simply a reminder for all of us to be aware of those who use figures to prove a point.

Thus far, we have dealt mainly with idealism and past historical events. We have covered the topics of freedom, liberty, individualism, and unity. I hope we are all on the same page insofar as these issues are concerned. As good Americans, regardless of political affiliation, we must honor and treasure these noble ideals.

Realistic thinking acknowledges the fact that there have been many changes over time in our demographics and such changes will continue long into the future. These changes necessitate adjustments to our thinking in order to accommodate the principles of democracy. More people equate to more rules, regulations, and restrictions.

We must acknowledge that strong force within many of us that yearns for the good old days. Most of us, at one time or other, have wished that we had done a few things differently in our lives. I have often wished that I had stayed in Colorado and had not accepted a significant promotion in California. But had that move not taken place, my children would not have met their spouses, and my grandchildren of today would not be the same people. I could not wish for better grandchildren. We must move onward! Only babies need to cry over spilled milk.

We must also remember that our forefathers were creating a new form of government. They were flying by the seat of their pants, making things up as they went along. To their credit, they made more right choices than wrong choices. Let us not fault them for shortcomings or shortsightedness but rather praise them for their noble efforts.

Switching back and forth between political ideologies indicates we are a house divided. We have learned little over the past seventy-five years. If we cannot learn from the past, there is little hope for the future. This brings us to the current administration, which will be a matter of discussion in part 2.

We must now live in the present with an eye focused on the future. Let us now give thought to the problems we face today. In closing this chapter, the following words of Patrick Henry (1736–1799) came to mind:

> "I have but one lamp by which my feet are guided, and that is the lamp of experience. I know no way of judging the future but by the past."

Shortly before Patrick Henry died he uttered these famous words:

> "United we stand, divided we fall."

PART 2

The Effects of the Past

Carryovers from the Past

The Obama Administration began under a cloud of fear because of the economic turmoil left behind by the previous administration. Many problems associated with the Great Depression had resurfaced. Large banks and insurance companies were in financial trouble. The stock market declined. The automobile industry was pleading for help. The housing market (the major cause and source of this economic meltdown) was collapsing, with foreclosures occurring in every neighborhood. Unemployment increased at an alarming rate. Mission kitchens were feeding thousands daily. The food stamp program was being exhausted. As baseball great Yogi Berra would have said: It was "déjà vu all over again"!

This negative set of circumstances took a turn for the worse during the waning days of the previous administration—occurring just before the presidential election of 2008. The outgoing administration, while trying to correct the situation, only made matters worse. The president-elect was in the midst of forming his new cabinet. Within weeks of the inauguration, he began to realize the magnitude of the negative situation that he was about to inherit. He was not given enough time to formulate a plan before the shoes began to drop in rapid succession.

Perhaps the incoming president could and/or should have declared some form of bank holiday as FDR did back in 1933. By freezing all the problems "in place," each problem could have been addressed—one at a time. This is called "Monday morning quarterbacking" on my part.

The problems associated with the automobile industry and the financial industry surfaced first—resulting in government bailouts. Had the automobile industry crumbled, a domino effect would have ensued in numerous related industries. The bailouts kept the automobile industry from going down the road toward bankruptcy. Those stopgap bailouts succeeded in that the negative ripple effects never took place. In the meantime, tens of thousands of individual families lost their homes, as the housing market continued to decline sharply. Many employed in the real estate and construction industries lost their jobs. Equity of millions of dollars was lost when housing prices dropped dramatically overnight.

Fewer citizens working and earning money resulted in fewer buyers of products. Fewer buyers resulted in layoffs within the retail and production sectors. Individual fears accelerated as the unemployment figures grew even higher. Could this terrible situation have been handled differently? Yes. However, when one considers how this rapidly developing situation was dumped onto this new president's lap, he performed quite well. The recovery process will be long and difficult, and there will be many hurdles to overcome. The blame game results in nothing worthwhile. The new president and his administration did not cause the problem. Those who did are no longer in power.

Many feel there should have been more strings attached to those early financial sector bailouts. As the primary culprits in the housing market failures, all executives of those organizations should have voluntarily taken a cut in salary. All bonuses, golden parachutes, buyouts, and other perks should have been suspended before anyone received even a penny's worth of government assistance. The shareholders of those same companies should have suffered some loss because of the inherent risk involved in all stock investments. For those who support pure, uncontrolled capitalism, stockholders of those institutions should have lost their collective shirts before involving the government. Even then, many homeowners were subjected to prolonged foreclosure proceedings because of government indecision.

The government was forced to become involved in this mess, and therefore it should have acted more decisively. This could have happened by insisting upon a moratorium on all foreclosures—resolving issues in a fair and equitable manner, case by case, if necessary. As a society, we do not wish to witness a large increase in homelessness. Our aim should have been to keep people in their homes and off the streets. The banking and insurance companies should have borne the cost, for they were the ones who caused the mess in the first place.

The adjustable mortgage rates (ARMs) along with so-called balloon payments were a major factor feeding this problem, and therefore they should have been curtailed or eliminated completely. That is to say, all ARMs should have been capped at a 2 percent increase or otherwise this concept in financing should have been eliminated completely. This cap should also apply to home equity loans wherein the agreed-upon interest rate should never drop below or advance beyond 2 percent. We need to reinstate and enforce usury laws. Financial institutions and loan sharks have much in common.

The next step should have been to convert as many ARMs as possible to affordable, fixed-rate mortgages. This would have built confidence in the future, plus it would have allowed individuals to remain in their homes. Every mortgage should have been reviewed in order to prevent speculators from profiting unnecessarily. This form of bailout should have applied only to owner-occupied housing.

Next, the government should have set an arbitrary 5 or 6 percent fixed interest rate on all qualifying foreclosure mortgages—at the same time allowing the terms of such mortgages to exceed thirty years. (Currently, few homeowners stay in one home for thirty years. The average age of the majority of loans is only eight years.) Increasing the term to fifty years would allow homeowners to achieve an affordable monthly payment and thus remain in their homes. This type of action would have avoided the current adverse effect on the overall housing market. As it now stands, all those who depended upon the value of their homes for future retirement purposes have lost substantial equity. As it now stands, every state must reassess property values, resulting in lost revenue for the state. The loss of state revenue could result in the layoff of teachers, policemen, firemen, etc. So much suffering caused by the greedy 1 or 2 percent!

Oh, well! What has been done has been done. As it now stands, the recovery will be slower and many more citizens will suffer in the interim. All of this points to the fact that government could resolve many economic issues without changing our form of government or switching to a different economic system.

Let those who clamor for free enterprise without government involvement, even when needed, come up with a better solution. The wealthy can continue to live comfortably while riding out such financial storms. The poor become even poorer. The middle class suffers the most during a downward economic spiral. Let us not attack the government for perhaps mishandling certain aspects of this meltdown. Let us blame those who knowingly caused the problem or were blinded by greed. We need to fix our economic system—more so than the government—in this regard.

The Presidency

The president of the United States—the most powerful job in the world. Or is it?

As Americans, we attribute a lot of importance to the presidency. Yet if we examine the position more closely, we might revise our thinking. Any current occupant of the White House is expected to know everything. He or she is either blamed or praised for everything that happens to our country during his or her administration. We seem to have glossed over the words in the Constitution concerning executive authority. The many checks and balances contained in that document can tie the hands of the president and make the position extremely weak. The job requires the help of the other two branches of government in order to make it a truly powerful position.

In reality, a president without such support from Congress can do little except defend our country and mess with the various agencies within the executive branch of government. Congress holds the purse strings. Without financial support, little can be accomplished. Every action taken by a president can be scrutinized by the Supreme Court in order to determine the constitutionality of such action.

So what is the presidency all about? If it had to be summarized in one word, that word would be *leadership*. In that regard, the president has the bully pulpit at his or her disposal. Consider this for a moment: we have capitalism as our economic system, wherein many believe government should not become involved in business. Why, then, is the president blamed when the unemployment figures are high? The president is not the hiring official for any large company or corporation within the private sector. He cannot change the payroll tax rates without the approval of Congress. So what can the president do besides plead for cooperation from the private sector and for money from Congress? When we hear campaign promises from presidential contenders who rant and rail against the sitting president, we should ask them for solutions based solely within the limits of their power if they should become president. It is not a matter of what they would like to do but rather what they legally *can* do. Without cooperation from Congress, there is little any president can accomplish.

The president is the representative of our country to the rest of the world. He or she should possess qualities that we can be proud of and foreigners can admire. A great president should be able to lift up our spirits during times of trial and tribulation. We must respect not only the office but also the person. Appearance means a lot, not necessarily in good looks, but in demeanor. There must be a strong element of intelligence involved. The person must exude honesty and confidence in order to be a good leader. Someone with a negative attitude should never be president. His or her morals should be high. The country's needs should come before self-interest. In summary, the president should be a leader who the people are not only willing but proud to follow.

The office of the president makes him or her commander in chief of the armed forces. He or she is called upon to defend this nation against all enemies, foreign and domestic. Currently terrorism has become a world enemy, and we must therefore formulate a different form of defense. We must know who is in our country at all times. For certain, we must remove all illegal aliens who have criminal records. The first order of business should be to secure our borders. The second order would be to identify everyone living within our borders. Once that was done, the president would be in a position to perform national defense duties in a responsible manner.

Elected officials are at the core of representative government. They are the voice of the people, reflecting the hopes and aspirations of the nation. We must select and elect persons who are honorable and trustworthy. Such traits are more important than affiliation with any political party. We can become beguiled by those with a "silver tongue" and overly impressed by academic achievements. We must continue to teach the story of the little boy who chopped down his father's cherry tree and the man named Honest Abe. Names like Tricky Dick and Slick Willy should never be applied to the president of our great country. Such negative comments reflect poorly on all the good citizens who put them in office.

Dare we now look closely at the current occupant of the White House? Can he speak well? Does he appear honest and sincere? Is he basically optimistic? Does he appear to want to move forward or does he wish to retreat into the bygone past? Is he well received by foreign leaders? Does he appear knowledgeable? Can he make tough decisions? Has he been connected to any form of scandal? How does he measure up in your mind? If he fails on all counts, the reader runs the risk of being called a bigot. If the reader feels the president needs to do better in certain areas, then he or she is normal and realistic. Everyone is allowed an opinion in a democracy. The president is just another human being—not necessarily a model of perfection, but rather a bearer of high standards.

The current president fought for a medical program that would ensure that all citizens had medical insurance coverage. The bill passed by Congress is far from perfect and not totally to the liking of the president, by his own admission. Many people are upset with this legislation. Some wished to repeal the law completely and start from scratch.

Allow me, as someone familiar with working within the confines and restraints of government, to make this observation. This is the key to getting things done in our country. It is extremely difficult to get a controversial law passed by both Houses. It requires a lot of compromise. Once a bill becomes law, it is easier to amend through compromise—bit by bit. (The Supreme Court ruled on June 28, 2012, that this law will not be repealed but requires modification.)

What needs to be done now is to enact changes to the law. Replace elements that are objectionable. Work out differences. Make the law the way it should be. If the health bill is a little sick, let us make it well! There are several good points within the current law—so let us be builders and move forward, making the law even better.

Much of the upcoming segment will be devoted to monetary issues. Let us begin by modifying that famous sign on former President Harry S. Truman's desk:

The Buck Starts Here

Economic Elements

The subject of economics is extremely complex. It is complex because it is difficult to find economists who totally agree with each other's point of view. There are dozens of theories afloat wherein so many renowned economists (such as Fisher, Friedman, Schwartz, Kindleberger, Eichengreen, and Temin) claim to have various solutions for handling financial problems. During the Great Depression, a British economist named John Maynard Keynes (1883–1946) presented his theory to the world. His hypothesis was to increase government involvement through stimulus spending (Does this sound familiar?), while at the same time lowering taxes. This is in sharp contrast to the current conservative viewpoint wherein both government spending and taxes are to be reduced at the same time, thereby—it is hoped— increasing production while decreasing the deficit.

Why is there so much disagreement concerning economics? Could it be that economics, being the creation of man, is subject to various opinions? Could customs, faith, traditions, beliefs, and other factors play a part in making this such a complex issue? Do more differences develop when we attempt to complicate our national economic system by trying to understand it and make it fit into a global system? The answer is a simple yes to all of these questions.

In order for us ordinary citizens to grasp certain economic principles, we must attack this massive subject one bite at a time. We must begin by separating domestic economic issues from global economic issues. In short, we must consider our own needs before we attempt to understand the needs of the world. We can best play the economic game with other nations once we learn the various complexities as they apply to our own situation.

Because the current economic situation is foremost on our minds, we will begin by discussing various financial matters. The reader will, I hope, make every effort to understand these elements fully within this upcoming presentation:

1. Money (specifically the US dollar)

2. The extraordinary benefits of, and need for, taxation

3. The author's "Domestic Spending Cycle"

4. The true effects of government spending on the deficit

5. The truth about the deficit

6. The unwarranted fears associated with a deficit

7. The effects of inflation

8. The importance of employment (either in government or

in the private sector), which is a vital component of our capitalistic system

These elements provoke disagreement, and many are interconnected, adding to the complexity of the overall issue. They are not in any particular order—they simply represent issues requiring more discussion and better understanding. These are elements we need to dissect thoroughly, one at a time, before proceeding to the next.

Money

Money stands at the core of most of our current political bickering. We argue over taxation, inflation, deficit spending, national debt, welfare benefits, subsidies, foreign aid, and the list goes on and on.

The coin of the realm was not necessarily a coin during our colonial period. The colonists used whatever was at hand to do business. Manhattan Island was bought from the local natives for what has been described as $24.00 worth of beads or wampum. In the southern colonies, the colonists used dried tobacco leaves as their form of currency. Those early settlers would accept doubloons from Spanish merchant ships and livres from French merchant ships, in addition to the pound, shilling, and pence used by the British merchants when doing business with other countries. Barter (that is, trading something in exchange for something else) was a common method for conducting commerce during the colonial period.

These comments are designed to help those who have an unwarranted fixation on the value of the dollar. We will attempt to be realistic when it comes to money. We must reduce the level of anxiety attributed to, or associated with, money.

At this point, it may be well to remind the reader that money is the invention of people. God had absolutely nothing to do with its creation. There is nothing spiritual or holy about money, even though we imprint "In God We Trust" on our currency and refer to it as the "Almighty Dollar."

Being an instrument of human beings, it is subject to the whims and will of humankind. To make this point, consider these many facts: (1) The US dollar was not in existence prior to 1792. How in the world did humankind exist before then? (2) The Germans once had money they called the Deutsche mark, the French had a franc, and the Italians had their lira, all of different monetary values. Today, these European countries use money called the euro, with a common value in all countries. (3) For many years, the English monetary system consisted of twelve pence to a shilling, and twenty shillings to a pound. They have since switched to a decimal system in which there are ten pence to a shilling and ten shillings to a pound, thereby making it easier for everyone to make change. (4) In the United States, our money was once backed by an amount in gold. Then we switched from a gold standard to issuing silver certificates. Now we can turn in a paper dollar bill and receive a Federal reserve note in exchange (this is called *fiat money*)—which makes no sense at all (swapping one piece of paper for another piece of paper). Right after World War II they used scrip (not unlike Monopoly money) in Europe in lieu of actual dollars. (5) Finally, the value of money (often referred to as buying power) has changed over the years, thanks to something called inflation.

Because we can make such changes whenever it is deemed necessary, there is nothing keeping us from switching back to wampum, should the need arise. Strange thought, isn't it? Strange but true! Such thoughts border on being sacrilegious in the eyes of fiscal conservatives. In fact, however, whatever is mutually agreed upon can be used as an acceptable currency.

For those who feel our money should be backed by a commodity such as gold, please consider these thoughts: Who determines the value of each bar of gold stored in Fort Knox? If the value (purchasing power) of the dollar is lowered through inflation, then the dollar amount of each gold bar increases with inflation. The overall weight of the gold remains unchanged.

Much of the world's gold is in the possession of our government, as reflected in the chart below. The most accepted currency in the world is the US dollar. In general, the world has agreed that our dollar is worth a stated value in their currency. We no longer back each dollar with a certain amount of gold or silver. Each dollar is currently backed by a promissory note. As long as these promissory notes have value in the eyes of all people, it is business as usual. It is our image as a nation that is at stake—our image gives us strength in the economic world and until recently we held a triple-A rating within the world financial system.

The recent antics of the so-called Tea Party helped to diminish our worldwide image and thus reduced our rating. This is another example of good intentions taking us down an undesirable path. If there is a perceived risk in lending money to our country, interest rates will rise, so that it costs us more to borrow money, and the deficit will increase more rapidly. Confidence instills trust and diminishes risks; thus lowering interest rates slows the growth of the deficit. It is unlikely that any member of the Tea Party will ever admit to doing anything wrong in this regard because of their myopic view regarding the deficit.

For those who place value on commodities, here are some figures regarding gold. The United States currently owns the largest gold reserves in the world:

Gold Reserves (2011)

1 USA	8,133.5 tonnes*
2 Germany	3,491.0
3 Int. Mon. Fund	2,846.7
4 Italy	2,451.8
5 France	2,435.4
6 China	1,054.1
7 Switzerland	1,040.1

*One tonne equals one metric ton.

When FDR took the United States off the gold standard, gold was selling for approximately $30 per ounce. (It is currently selling at more than $1,600 per ounce). It fluctuates with inflation and with the value of the dollar. No other country has more of this commodity than we do. To the gold reserve we could add our silver reserves, more precious metals, gems, oil and coal reserves, plus other commodities to determine national wealth.

National wealth and financial well-being are expressed in several different ways. The Gross Domestic Product and Wealth per Capita are two such ways. There should be no doubt in anyone's mind after reading these figures that the United States is the wealthiest nation in the world. Here are a few more figures to consider:

Gross Domestic Product (2011)

1 United States	$15,060,000
2 China	7,000,000
3 Japan	6,000,000
4 Germany	3,600,000

Wealth per Capita (2011)

1 Luxembourg
3 Norway
7 United States

Oil-producing countries
complete the top ten listing.

Currently, the world uses money (not gold) as its acceptable medium of exchange. Should the day ever come when the dollar is considered worthless by the masses, our economy would suffer dramatically.

George Washington named Alexander Hamilton to be the first Secretary of the Treasury in 1792. It was Hamilton who selected the economic system called capitalism to be the economic engine for our new country. He could have just as easily recommended a different economic system, and today most of us would be none the wiser. Capitalism is not mentioned in the Constitution or in any of the Amendments.

The point being, we would still be a democratic republic—even if we used a different economic system.

This would be a good opportunity to introduce the concept and a brief historical background of capitalism.

Various elements of capitalism have been with humankind for more than two thousand years. (The ancient Phoenician merchants understood the principles of supply and demand.) It was a Scottish economist named Adam Smith (1723–1790) who introduced a more formal theory of capitalism to the world in 1760. This was in the early days of the Industrial Revolution and near the time of our Declaration of Independence. His theory was based mainly on rural communities with relatively small entrepreneurs (cottage industries) dominating commerce. He had no way of foretelling that giant global corporations would one day control commerce. Had he been able to see into the future, he would have more than likely made a few changes to his original theory. Currently, Adam Smith's pure version of capitalism is unlikely to exist anywhere on this planet. Various modifications to his original theory of capitalism have taken place on a worldwide scale over these many years.

Hamilton felt that capitalism would best serve the needs of our new nation. The theory mixes well with individualism and free enterprise. It provided equality of opportunity. It rewarded hard work and creativity. Hamilton has been referred to as "the patron saint" of the American school of economic philosophy. As a member of the Federalist Party, he strongly advocated a centralized banking system and was opposed to each state having its own banking system. (Try to imagine fifty different $10 bills.)

Basic capitalism served our country extremely well during the early days of our nation's existence. It could continue to serve our needs best for many more years *if* we understand a major flaw in the original theory. In Adam Smith's original theory, government was to play a very minor role in the economy. He allowed for some government involvement but basically felt that the natural principles of supply and demand would be the best stabilizing factors in developing a successful economic system.

His new but untried theory worked well enough until the natural greed within humankind began to surface and overwhelm the system. It has now become a case of too much of a good thing. "It takes money to make money," as the saying goes. Those with too much discretionary income become unsatisfied with having only millions of dollars—they now want to acquire billions.

Capitalism is creating a class system within our society. We are developing both an ever-growing rich society while enlarging the poor sector (which obviously results in the shrinking of the middle class). This is contrary to the principles of a democracy but in keeping with the principles defining a republic. We can continue on this path, or we can modify the course on which uncontrolled capitalism will take us. We, the people (as stated in our founding documents), can bring about such change, should we so desire. At present there is no need to switch economic systems, but we must control the one we have. We must contain the evil associated with greed. It must be "all for one" (as in unity) and not "all for one" (as in greed).

The easiest and most enlightened fix for this situation is to involve government more than Adam Smith suggested. Government rules, regulations, oversights, caps, etc., will be needed to curb the greedy, as they cannot control themselves. With needed safeguards in place, the main essence of capitalism can be maintained. We can continue to enjoy the great aspects of this economic system for many more years and, at the same time, enjoy the blessings of democracy.

Our failure to take remedial action will eventually result in the collapse of our great nation. We need not worry about foreign aggressors, for we will undo ourselves! The present-day marches on Wall Street are but a beginning of civil economic unrest. These citizens are tired of playing cutthroat Monopoly. They are seeking a new edition of an old game that seemed to have worked well back in the 1930s. FDR called it a "New Deal." We must take his concept, make much-needed updates, and continue forward. We must reshuffle the deck—place caps and restrictions on the high rollers and remove all wild cards.

With such safeguards in place, there should be no need to experience a monetary meltdown every other generation. If we make no change, history will repeat itself. It is time for us to make a choice—to exercise our freedom.

The passage of time often creates a need for change!

Taxation

Another major aspect of American economics is taxation. Taxation has been with mankind for centuries: "And it came to pass in those days, that there went out a decree from Caesar Augustus, that all the world should be taxed" (Luke 2:1). Caesar Augustus must have been a Democrat! All joking aside, there are two vastly different views concerning the issue of taxation in America. The majority view is the simple hatred of taxation in any form. The minority view considers taxation a necessary evil.

Both views consider waste and misappropriations as being wrong. Such things add to the negative view held by the majority. The majority view is quite understandable, as it is so basic to human nature—everyone dislikes paying taxes. One merely has to mention the word "taxes," and people begin to grumble! There really is no need to discuss negativity toward taxation, so let us examine the minority view in greater detail in order to obtain a more appropriate and realistic understanding of the subject.

Picture yourself sitting in an expensive sports car capable of breaking the sound barrier. You were able to afford this vehicle because you no longer had to pay taxes. But because of no taxation, there would be huge potholes in the pavement in all the streets and roads—that is, if there were any pavement at all. And, by the way, there would be nothing that would pass for a highway anywhere in the country. Your personal, well-maintained driveway is less than one hundred feet long. Sigh! All that zoom-zoom and nowhere to zoom!

Picture yourself standing on any corner in any major city. You are wearing a fashionable and expensive suit or dress that you bought with your tax savings. The roadway is without pavement, there are no sidewalks or gutters, and it looks like it is about to rain. Sigh! Save on taxes, and spend more at the dry cleaners!

Picture yourself living in a beautiful hilltop home with a fantastic view, which you can now afford without taxation. The neighbors below complain every time you flush your toilet, as there are no sewers, and septic tanks have a limited capacity. Besides, you don't want to flush very often anyway—as it takes a lot of effort to haul the water up from a low-lying well or creek. There is no city water to flow through the nonexistent water and sewer systems. Sigh! Oh well—they do deliver bottled water to your home. And once the rainy season begins, there will be plenty of water for bathing.

Picture yourself in a wonderful, fully-equipped RV pulling into Yellowstone Park, thanks again to not having to pay taxes. The park isn't really a park, but a once-beautiful wilderness area created by God. Now beer and pop cans can be seen everywhere! The outhouse is a slit in the dirt and has attracted flies from fifty miles away. Sigh! A place of pristine beauty is beginning to look more like a landfill.

Life in the United States is far better in the material sense than in any other country in the world. The main difference can be found in the infrastructure that serves the needs of all citizens. Look around! Much of the infrastructure is brought about by taxation, coupled to rules and regulations.

Taxation is a good thing when citizens receive something of value in return for their money. Taxation is a bad thing when the money is wasted or lines the pockets of corrupt individuals. Taxation is but an expression of unity! We pool our resources and get things done.

Without this team effort, life would be primitive and dismal.

Now let us examine taxation through the eyes of two major political philosophies: conservative and progressive. The conservative view consists of four major elements involving tax reduction and limited government spending:

1. Conservatives believe that, with more of our own money in our hands, we will spend more, thus stimulating the overall economy—a principle often referred to as trickle-down economics. (There is an element of truth to this belief.)

2. When government spends less than it takes in, the deficit decreases, thus saving our children and grandchildren from economic ruin in the future. (There is also an element of truth to this belief.)

3. Government rules and regulations stifle growth, which hampers the wheels of capitalism from turning freely. These rules and regulations take away from humankind's freedom. (This is not always the case.)

4. As the rich acquire more wealth, they will not only spend more (in theory), thus creating more jobs—they will invest in creating more enterprises. (This too is not always true.)

It has often been said that the poor will always be with us. Because many people have limited mental and physical capacities, such statements have validity. We are created equal, but differences develop at birth and continue throughout life. Those of us who are more blessed should consider the following, not as a religious quotation, but rather a sound humanitarian philosophy: "For unto whomsoever much is given, of him shall be much required" (Luke 12:48). The least capable citizens are the least capable of improving their position in life! We who are more blessed must care for such individuals or become heartless by ignoring their plight. What does your heart tell you? Are you cold-hearted and cynical? Are you in life only for yourself? Are you among the greedy?

Progressive thinkers understand the conservative position completely. There is no misunderstanding, but rather a difference of opinion how to best answer the needs of our people and at the same time be true to the spirit of our Constitution and the Bill of Rights, which is aimed toward equality. Armed with these ideological beliefs, the progressive goal is to enhance the principles of the *common good* while trying to avoid the creation of a class system. As such, the progressive position favors actions that promote a very strong economic middle class rather than "a have and a have-not" society. The progressive position has been weakened because of failure to follow through by explaining the rationale and specifics behind their proposals. The progressive position is on the right track, but it must show their fellow citizens why they are on the right track.

Taxing individuals based on their ability to pay has merit. Taxing individuals based on their *inability* to pay makes no (cents) sense. A bigger house equates to higher property taxes. A more expensive car equates to higher sales and personal property taxes—so why not tax larger incomes accordingly? The more progressive quest to create a better country for the majority middle class requires government involvement.

Many self-satisfied, wealthy citizens give little thought to the needs of others. Not all wealthy individuals are heartless. Many are philanthropists who give generously to worthy causes—such individuals deserve recognition and praise. Unfortunately, the greedy outnumber those who have a more humanitarian outlook on life. We must keep in mind the attitude of the former French queen Marie Antoinette when told that her people had no bread to eat. She arrogantly replied, "Then let them eat cake!" This was said just before she was beheaded by her hungry citizens. (She then had cake but could not eat it!) Any form of a future revolution will not be in the best interests of the wealthy. (Look at the more recent history of Brazil as a shining example.)

The progressive movement should express the following thoughts in order to select the best course of action for our country:

1. When citizens are employed, they pay taxes. When citizens are not employed, they pay no taxes, plus they add to the deficit by receiving unemployment benefits or food stamps.

2. The unemployed pay nothing into retirement funds and the Medicare program, thus weakening the future solvency of those trust funds.

3. Employment is the best way to stimulate the economy and thus lessen the negative aspects associated with the deficit. This applies to both private sector and government employment.

4. If the employment is with the government, it should result in improvements for society. In other words, government spending should be aimed at making our overall standard of living better. We currently enjoy the best standard of living the world has ever known, but it could be even better.

5. Unfortunately, no one company in the private sector can make that happen. For example: the principal funding for the space program came from government, not from any private source. Risk and profitability play a major factor in keeping private funding from joining the government in aerospace research and development. Government foresight and taxation got us to where we are today. Do we Americans lack a good measure of self-esteem? Have we forgotten that our government is "we the people"? Rather than damn the government, stand up and take a bow.

It is only government, by pooling resources and working together (unity and taxation), that can improve the overall national standard of living by advancing projects that might not show a profit at the time of their conception.

Thus far, we have been discussing individual taxation and not corporate taxation. As ordinary citizens, we have more personal involvement in individual taxation. Corporate taxation represents a different and more complex can of worms. As of this writing, on paper we have the highest corporate tax rate (35 percent) of any industrialized nation. In reality, corporations in this country pay one of the lowest corporate tax rates (more like 17 percent) in the industrial world. Only companies that do not employ competent accountants and tax attorneys pay higher rates. The current corporate tax code is so complex, with so many loopholes, that it requires a "Philadelphia lawyer" in order to prepare the necessary paperwork. Could the code be simplified? Yes—through legislation! Will it happen? Over the dead bodies of the lobbyists!

Even the individual tax code could be simplified. Take, for example, the exemptions given for each member of the household—the more children (exemptions), the greater the tax reduction. Here is the irony of this situation: more children will increase the need for more schools and teachers who are paid out of tax revenue. The single person or those couples without children pay more taxes to subsidize the children of large families. The fairest method for correcting this situation would be to do away with all personal exemptions. Such action would increase tax revenue overall, or the current tax rate could be lowered. Our population has grown over the years, and therefore the need to enhance or encourage the birthrate has passed.

Here is a current population assessment of the five largest countries in the world. The percentage of world population is shown. China and India dwarf the United States in this comparison:

World Population (2011)

1 China	1,347,350,000	19.2%
2 India	1,210,193,422	17.3%
3 USA	313,338,000	4.5%
4 Indonesia	237,641,326	3.4%
5 Brazil	192,376,496	2.8%

Another section of the tax code could be simplified, as it pertains to itemized versus standard deductions. Eliminating the itemized deduction would increase revenue. Eliminating both the itemized and standard deductions would increase revenue even more. Eliminate both and simply adjust (downward) the tax rates on the taxable income charts. (Think of all the lines that could be eliminated from Form 1040.)

If anyone enjoys thinking outside the box, they are going to love this next segment. I cannot verify the fact that this is an original thought; however, I have never found anyone who has proposed arguments along this line. Perhaps I am hanging out with the wrong crowd!

The Domestic Spending Cycle (DSC)

The Domestic Spending Cycle (DSC) is a unique approach to understanding the American economic system. Most Americans live from payday to payday. They earn their paycheck, budget their priorities, and spend accordingly. Little thought is given to every dollar once it leaves their hands. The Domestic Spending Cycle simply follows each dollar in order to determine its effect on our economic system.

To appreciate the following discussion, the reader first needs to understand fully the concept of the Domestic Spending Cycle. Each of those three words has a specific meaning that will become apparent as we continue.

We begin by acknowledging payroll and other forms of taxation. When an individual citizen earns money, he or she pays a whole series of taxes: federal and state (perhaps even local) income taxes—followed by various payroll taxes, such as Social Security, Medicare Part A, etc. Let us not forget sales taxes, personal property taxes, along with various user and excise taxes. It has been said that we all work from January 1 to mid-May each year just to pay these various forms of taxation—that is nearly 40 percent of our work time! Let us use this 40 percent in the following example, as we delve deeper into the concept of the Domestic Spending Cycle.

A citizen performs a service as a private contractor for the federal government and earns $1,000. Using the above 40 percent figure, he would end up paying back to the government $400 in taxes, which leaves him with $600 to spend as he sees fit. He hires a plumber to fix the pipes and fittings around his home and pays the plumber $600 for services rendered. The plumber pays 40 percent of this income ($240) in taxes, which leaves him with $360 to spend. The plumber hires an electrician for $360 to fix wiring problems at his house. The electrician pays 40 percent ($144) in taxes, which leaves him with $216. Continue this process until the last dime has been paid to some individual. You will note that, through some form of taxation, the government has recovered the amount originally paid to the first contractor.

The point being that if all money is spent within our country, (this is where the word *Domestic* takes on meaning), our government will eventually reclaim the original $1,000 in some form of taxation. What started out as deficit spending becomes a moot point. It matters not if the employee is a government worker or someone in the private sector.

It matters little if the original employer was the government or some company within the private sector. The key for the positive aspect of the Domestic Spending Cycle to work is that all purchases and expenditures stay within the borders of our country. There is an old saying when investigating white-collar crimes: "Follow the money." The DSC is but an adaptation of that principle.

We must follow each dollar in order to see how it travels throughout the country. Individual dollars pass through multiple hands, serving the needs of many along the way. (The word *Cycle* now takes on meaning.) The cycle is broken when the dollar leaves our shores or when it is taken out of circulation. Money under a mattress or forever lost or destroyed is money no longer in circulation. (Money not in circulation ceases to be spending money—thus giving emphasis to the word *Spending*.)

Now let us look at another spending situation. Many entitlement program payments such as Medicare will end up in a doctor's or a hospital employee's paycheck, and the cycle will continue. The money paid to Social Security recipients will be spent at the drugstore or the food market, and the cycle continues. Every dollar spent is part of the cycle as long as it is spent within our economic system. If dollars are spent in some other country, then that country places those dollars within their cycle, and we subtract a loss of actual dollars from our system. It is these lost dollars—not simply government spending—that drive up the deficit.

It might be best to give one more example of how the DSC works, as it might appear more complex as the money begins to spread out to multiple hands. Let us begin by spending $100 at the local grocery store, since everyone has to eat. The grocer pays his suppliers (various canneries); pays his utility bills (overhead costs); pays his employees; and keeps the rest for himself. It is easy to see the DSC at work in terms of employee salaries and his own take-home pay.

Now let us look at the money given to the supplier. The supplier (cannery) pays for the tin to make the cans; then pays the farmer for the peas; then pays his utility bills; and then pays his employees before keeping a little something for himself.

The farmer pays for his seed and fertilizer. He maintains his farm equipment; pays his utility bills; and lives off the fat of the land and by the sweat of his brow.

The folks working for the various utility companies have to be paid in order to feed their families and the cycle continues.

Is the reader beginning to grasp the full concept of the DSC? The national deficit can best be controlled by our keeping spending dollars within our system. Overseas spending is the major cause of our ever-growing deficit. We consumers, when buying foreign products, are adding more to the deficit than simple government spending, as proclaimed by those who call themselves fiscal conservatives. There are many ways, other than the trade imbalance, in which foreign spending affects our deficit.

In the past, we have been admonished to "Buy American." This was originally a call to support unionism. This call must be updated! The call should be more restricted and changed to "Buy USA." In their attempt to beguile us, car manufacturers and others like to tout the phrase "Made in America," which includes Mexico and Canada. Foreign paychecks will not be included within the DSC. Those dollars are gone, and our national deficit grows.

We cannot stop all losses. According to official government records, a small percentage (nearing 1 percent) of all Social Security benefits are sent abroad. Many individuals come to America to find employment before retiring to their native lands. Such overseas annuities are averaging nearly $20,000 per year. This represents a loss of nearly half a billion dollars per year from our DSC through this source alone.

Where we shop could enhance our overall well-being. Small entrepreneurs are the backbone of any economy. By supporting local businesses, bedroom communities become stronger. The taxes from these small, local businesses help offset local residential property taxes. (You need only ask the local chamber of commerce to verify that statement.) Purchases over the Internet generally represent a loss to a local community. The product shown on the Internet may have been made in a foreign land. The party selling the item may not even be in the United States. Shopping at large discount stores can cause similar negative results. When considering the cost of gasoline, shopping at a local store may actually be more cost effective. The tighter and more localized the domestic spending, the more the consumer will benefit in the long run.

What has been stated thus far in this segment may be considered too simplistic. It was meant to be so! Many would cloud financial issues with incomprehensible jargon shrouding the subject in mystifying terms. The reader is urged to review the concept of the DSC very carefully. A reader might justifiably question the 40 percent taxation rate, for in some states there is no sales tax or the sales tax rate might vary from state to state. Change the taxation rate to some lesser percentage, and it will simply add another cycle or two toward the ultimate outcome. Try not to get hung up on petty issues—it is the main thought that counts. We would be a financially stronger group of people if we kept our money within our family. Perhaps we should call such thoughts "common cents"!

Government Spending

According to economic conservatives, government spending plays an important role in increasing our deficit. Let us take a quick peek at the federal budget as it relates to the DSC. A large percentage of tax revenue goes to entitlement programs; another large percentage goes toward defense department expenditures; while yet another sum is applied towards miscellaneous administrative activities.

A very substantial part of these three groupings involves the payment of benefits and/or salaries—both civilian and military, at all levels of government. The majority of such payments fall within the concept of the DSC. All entitlement benefits will eventually fall within the concept of the DSC, as those beneficiaries will spend their money in the normal course of living. The vast majority of all government purchases from the private sector for goods and services will end up in the DSC. The same applies to all taxes paid to the various states and local governments. Once money from any source becomes spending money, it becomes part of the DSC.

The payment of interest on our national debt to foreign governments or individuals has an adverse effect on the DSC. Foreign debt needs to be minimized as much as possible.

The unnecessary deployment of our military troops overseas likewise feeds the deficit. It may be necessary for US Marines to be stationed in our embassies throughout the world for the protection of our diplomats and property. It is not necessary, however, to maintain thousands of military personnel in Japan, Korea, Germany, Italy, and England. Those service personnel, along with their dependents, spend US dollars in those foreign lands. Such expenditures help those foreign countries, while adding to our deficit. We should close overseas bases and relocate those service personnel somewhere within the United States if we wish to reduce the deficit. While the government is spending money, regardless of the location of its military personnel, the national deficit is lessened if those salaries remain within the boundaries of the United States.

The author spent two years in midtown London as a young US sailor. The navy could not provide government housing, so in addition to a normal sailor's salary, I received an extraordinary foreign-living allowance. Talk about a plush duty assignment! There were so many of us—we could not wear our uniforms to work for fear the English would think they were being invaded. (Try to imagine a sea of white hats among a sea of bowler hats!) This expenditure supported a land-based admiral who could perform the same duties in a less expensive area. Thanks to the generous taxpayers in America, a good time was had by all. This is an example of military waste and yet another example of unnecessary deficit spending. I have recently been told that this command might be relocated to Italy. At least the admiral will be closer to some ships. For the purpose of this discussion nothing significant will be changed.

Today (this information is available on the Internet), according to official records there are approximately 10,000 US service personnel serving in the United Kingdom. What for? There are more than 150,000 military personnel currently serving on foreign soil (not including war zones). Why? Many of these military personnel have their families with them. Many live in off-base housing. While many shop in a military commissary, many items purchased in the commissary are provided by local businesses (e.g., milk, bread, eggs, fresh fruits, and meats, etc.). These purchases remove money from the DSC. Maybe we should allow friendly foreign governments to set up military bases in our country for a fee. Currently our military expenditures overseas represent taxpayer money being spent without reciprocity. This is deficit spending, pure and simple.

The misguided use of foreign aid can likewise adversely affect our deficit. Foreign aid will be a topic of discussion later on in this book. Our assistance to other nations should be limited so as to have the least negative effect on our deficit.

Many illegal aliens add to our deficit in numerous ways. Illegal (as well as legal) aliens can add to our growing deficit by sending some of what they earn here in the United States back to their families in their native lands. One may sympathize with their motives. One can appreciate their concern for their families back home. Nevertheless, money leaving our borders is money removed from our domestic spending cycle. It is estimated there are more than eleven million such illegal aliens (and this may not include all those who have crossed over the Canadian border) living in the United States. The overall subject of illegal aliens will likewise be a major topic of discussion later on in this book as it affects many other aspects of life here in the United States.

Understanding the concept of the Domestic Spending Cycle should afford a more enlightened view as to a major cause of our national deficit. Overall government spending is not the driving force that causes the deficit to grow. Internal government spending can be used as a stimulus for our overall economy and well-being. External spending by both the official government and "we the people" as consumers are the main cause of the deficit. If one worries about the deficit, one should stop spending money on foreign purchases. We should not shackle our government by insisting that all spending (foreign and domestic) be curtailed. There is a strong correlation between the effects of the Domestic Spending Cycle and the deficit. Now let us turn our attention toward various aspects of the deficit.

Deficit

Is critical thinking a lost art in the United States of America? So many Americans worry needlessly over deficit spending and the ever-increasing national debt. As stated above, domestic spending is generally considered a good thing.

Ultraconservative groups perpetrate fear by claiming that future generations will be saddled with a national debt so large that it will somehow destroy life as we know it. They want to sound "retreat" by cutting government spending and lowering taxes in order to stimulate the economy. We need to look at this matter in greater detail, exploring concepts that will put the national debt in proper perspective.

The very first year that we had an operational government was 1788, when George Washington was our president. A review of our historical economic records (information that is readily available on the Internet) will prove that since then we have had a yearly deficit under all but two presidential administrations (Andrew Jackson and William Jefferson Clinton). Ironically, both were Democrats, who are generally believed to be big government spenders. Jackson not only operated his administration within the confines of his budget; he was the only president who ever paid down the national debt. Clinton only managed to operate within the limits of his budget, thereby not adding to the national debt. All other administrations have run up the national debt—some more so than others.

During war years the deficit will understandably grow more rapidly. President Reagan, ironically an ultraconservative Republican, during his (war-free) administration, broke all peacetime deficit records. We should take away from this information the fact that deficits have been with us since the beginning, regardless of political considerations. There is nothing new about the concept of deficits. Our country (the wealthiest on the planet) has managed to exist quite well since 1788, even with deficits. Could it be that deficits are not as bad as we are being led to believe? Could it be that overall government spending is not the main cause of a growing deficit?

Is a national debt something we should lose sleep over? FDR had an expression that has a meaning worthy of thoughtful consideration: "We owe it to ourselves!" Can we rationally compare the national debt to our own personal debt? As individuals, can we owe ourselves money? If so, who is going to hunt us down for repayment? Who will be calling us in the middle of the night demanding payment? What would actually go into foreclosure if we were to default on a debt to ourselves? Can we now better appreciate and understand FDR's words?

Many cynics like to say, "If I ran my business the way the government operates, I would be put in jail." (Maybe it's because individuals cannot be trusted!) For those who would like to compare government spending to their own personal budgets, please consider the following thoughts:

In the private sector, bookkeepers and accountants routinely prepare what is called a balance sheet, on which assets should be equal to, or greater than, liabilities. If assets are greater than liabilities, then the business is said to be running in the black. Such a business is said to be healthy. Individually, we might refer to this as our net worth—when we own more than what we owe.

Now keep in mind ordinary bookkeeping practices when considering the following facts: the US government still holds title to more than 20 percent of all land within our borders. That land has a far greater value than all the gold and silver currently found in Fort Knox. As for current assets, bookkeepers would have to conduct an annual inventory of assets in order to place a value on all items owned by any individual company or person in order to determine net worth. By using the same criteria when auditing government assets, bookkeepers would have to include the value of all federally owned buildings, post offices, airfields, military bases, cars, trucks, tanks, ships, aircraft, computers, typewriters, pens, and pencils. It is the view of many economists that our national assets outweigh our national debt.

Please remember, the amount of our official national debt is stated in fiat dollars—not in any other commodity. (Fiat currency is created by authority [through decree] and is not necessarily backed by any form of security. It is little more than paper chasing paper!) When China loans us money, they do so by using our fiat dollars, which they gained through our trade deficit. They do not use their own yuan. The interest they earn will be paid in fiat dollars, not in any other commodity.

American companies want to do business with China. China represents a large market in which to sell their products and make company profits. Do these American companies worry about the overall American trade deficit? Not in the least! That is for the government to worry over. This is uncontrolled capitalism at work—where the company's bottom line is more important than any national consideration. This has nothing to do with our being a democratic republic. It has more to do with our capitalistic economic system being a breeding ground for greed.

Returning to our discussion of bookkeeping practices—in the private sector, many businesses close their shops and factories for a day or two each year in order to conduct an inventory. This sort of thing doesn't happen within the vastness of government for obvious reasons. For the government it falls within the realm of trust. So let us stop making ridiculous comparisons between individual or private sector bookkeeping and government bookkeeping practices. If we applied basic bookkeeping terms to our country's financial stability, we would be operating in the black. Such an approach renders the deficit meaningless.

Here is another factor we should consider when we discuss future increases in the deficit: if, as a nation, we put off making necessary repairs to our infrastructure to avoid increasing the deficit, we are overlooking the fact that future generations will have to pay more to fix those same problems at a later date. This is the inevitable aftermath of the inflation factor!

Would future interest charges offset the amount caused by present-day spending? (Spend now and pay more interest later versus do nothing now and pay higher repair costs later.) The old adage, "Penny-wise and pound-foolish!" may well apply in this situation. By delaying needed repairs, we become more vulnerable to experiencing safety problems during the interim, such as collapsing bridges, etc. (Example: St. Paul, Minnesota, southbound Interstate Highway 35, bridge over the Mississippi River collapsed on August 1, 2007, causing four deaths, seventy-nine injuries, and leaving twenty missing. Putting things off only delays the inevitable and could result in tragic events like this.) Would the members of the Tea Party—and those who think like them—like to take credit for this avoidable accident?

For those concerned about the well-being of future generations: they should worry more about today's environmental issues, which will have a greater impact on future generations, than the deficit. If we spend money today to improve our environment, we would be benefiting both present and future generations. If we spend our money wisely—by keeping our air, water, and soil clean and productive—future generations will bless us. We must become good stewards over those limited resources. We should not be wasteful and careless, but let us be more realistic. Investing for today is, in fact, investing in the future, because today ushers in tomorrow.

Many citizens worry about the amount of money other countries and foreigners have invested in our country. These foreigners have purchased our bonds, and some have bought choice properties within the United

States. Is this a legitimate worry? Could such investors cause our country to collapse? Let us view a negative scenario for a moment.

What would we do if a large foreign country called in their loans? Our options are many! We could pay them with fiat money (thereby increasing the rate of inflation). Perhaps we could give them some gold and/or silver bars stored in Fort Knox (highly unlikely). Or maybe we could give them the Utah Salt Flats or part of the Mojave Desert and demand they take all that sand and salt with them when they leave. (Impossible—I'm kidding, of course!)

Realistically, real property cannot leave our shores. Foreign ownership of property can be controlled and regulated by our government at the state level. The worst foreign investors could do, would be to cut all future investment ties with us. Would they go to war over money? Unlikely, as that would cost more than what we owe them! As with many investments, investors bear a burden of risk! If, as individuals, we invest in a company by purchasing their stock, and that company should go into bankruptcy, who suffers? It is those individuals who hold the stocks or bonds. The foreign investor assumes a degree of risk when loaning money to our government. Currently they are willing to take that risk.

Why do so many foreign companies and countries invest in the United States? They do so because we are the safest place in the world for investment. Why doesn't China invest heavily in Chad, Libya, Congo, Greece, Spain, Egypt, Syria, or Cuba? It is because these countries have less than stable governments, which offer no guarantee and little promise regarding foreign investments. We are the world's safe haven for sound investments. All we must do is remain calm, stable, and united. If anyone can find a safer haven, they should invest in it. Keep in mind—should we fail, the rest of the world will be right behind us.

There are many ways of tackling concerns over deficits and the ever-present national debt. Some ways are more productive than others. Manipulating tax rates and/or cutting government spending for fiscal conservatives is the most obvious way, yet such tactics are often the least effective and often counterproductive. A more meaningful way to reduce the deficit would be to apply the principles of the Domestic Spending Cycle.

Tea Party thinkers please take note: tying the hands of government when no privately owned company or corporation is capable of coming to the economic aid of the country is counterproductive.

The furloughing of government employees is likewise counterproductive, since the unemployed: (1) pay no taxes; (2) buy little to stimulate the economy; (3) and draw unemployment checks that further hamper attempts to achieve a balanced budget. Let us not forget that, while people are unemployed, they are not paying into Social Security or Medicare, and this weakens the financial stability of those programs in the future.

As a people, we tend to worry more than necessary. People who have nothing to lose worry the least. So let us take a moment to discuss:

The Fear Factor

When I think about fear, I am reminded of my early childhood. During those formative years I was raised by a very generous and loving aunt. Unable to have children of her own, she set about spoiling me to no end. She was a devoutly religious person with high morals and a charitable soul.

Notwithstanding her good qualities, she was filled with fear and anxiety. Her phobias were almost without number. I must tell you about two of her phobias.

She never learned to drive an automobile, yet she loved to go for car rides, provided that her husband was the driver. She trusted him completely but felt unsafe in the hands of others. Making a left turn at any busy intersection would cause her to have an acute attack of anxiety. She felt the oncoming traffic would crash into her side of the car and either kill or maim her. Rather than put her through this agony, my uncle would pass by the desired intersection and make a series of right turns in order to achieve his ultimate destination. The family would smirk and giggle every time this happened. We all joked that the car would fall apart if it ever made a left turn. (By the way, my uncle was a Democrat!)

The second phobia would emerge as the result of violent thunder and lightning storms—common occurrences in the Chicago area. My aunt would immediately pull down the shades and close the drapes. She would light a candle for each room and then take out her prayer beads and begin reciting her rosary quite rapidly. She approached a state of panic each time lightning illuminated the room, or there was a loud clap of thunder. The family would again smirk and giggle. Here was a God-fearing woman actually fearing God.

This was a wonderful person—with hang-ups. Before leaving the house, she would repeatedly check every door and window to make certain it was closed and locked. Everything had to be just so, with nothing out of place. Flying in an airplane was out of the question. Perhaps as a result of all this, I had to outgrow many personal phobias. My greatest phobia concerned dogs. I would cross the street rather than go near a dog. I would begin to sweat if the dog showed its teeth or began to bark. I overcame that fear by getting a small puppy, learning the ways of a canine, and growing old with it. At present I have a rather large dog constantly by my side. She will grab my arm with her mouth in play, never so much as scratching my skin. My fear of dogs has been replaced by a true understanding of what it means to be "man's best friend."

Most humans have fears or phobias. Fear is often devoid of realism. We have worries and doubts. The unknown is often the cause of anxiety. All this is normal as we cope with learning what life is all about. Economic fears and the fear of a Big Brother government taking over our lives are common fears, which cause me to smirk and giggle.

Having said all this, I cannot help but remember the words of FDR: "We have nothing to fear, but fear itself." Let us put the fear of the ever-increasing deficit on the back burner while concentrating on current needs. Allow the next generation to cope with the problems they will face, just as our forefathers and our generation did in the past and in the present. Life will go on with or without a deficit! If right-wing extremists cannot trust my thinking concerning the deficit, then let them follow the example of Ronald Reagan for a reality check. (I promise not to smirk and giggle.)

The best way to reduce the deficit is to place the burden on other countries. Here are a few ways to achieve such a goal:

1. Strive to reduce our trade deficit—the major cause of our national deficit.
2. Apply the principles outlined in the Domestic Spending Cycle to compensate for the formal trade imbalance.
3. Through taxation, restrict outsourcing of jobs by American companies.
4. Terminate excessive overseas deployment of our military personnel.
5. Restrict foreign aid as outlined below.
6. Remove illegal aliens from our country.

Many will claim that some of these suggested courses of action will lead to isolationism or protectionism—thereby building a "fortress America." To be honest—our government has entered into so many trade agreements that it cannot officially support the notions put forth in this book. This is a matter for citizens who care about their country. This is a matter for citizens who put their country first. We are suffering trade deficits because the peoples of other countries are doing unto us before we get a chance to do it unto them.

Let us expand upon the points outlined above.

Trade deficits represent money leaving our country and helping the economies of other countries. We have been and are currently being shortchanged in this regard, year after year.

Why is it called free trade when we are the ones bearing the financial burden?

As a sub issue, any imbalance in tourism should be included in this draining of resources. Citizens who travel overseas spend dollars. Tourists who visit this country bring their currency to our shores. Currently, we do more visiting than hosting. We could, of course, spend more time touring our own country, rather than traveling abroad. It would be even better if we had more foreign tourists visiting our country.

As a relatively young country, we lack the history and charm of the Old World and the exotic settings of the Far East. What can we do about this form of economic shortfall? Each state might compile a complete record of its most mundane happenings within various counties and towns. (This is being done in many places, thanks to the efforts of local chapters of the chamber of commerce and various historical societies.) We should intensify these efforts in order to make our local communities sound more worthy of a visit. We should try to maintain the oldest buildings in town as part of a local history. As Americans, we have a tendency to bulldoze old buildings and pave the ground with cement—all in the name of modernization.

We need to create stories about the history of the area and make it sound interesting. Embellishments would be allowed! In short, promote tourism with the hope that visitors will leave some of their money behind. Has the reader ever visited the Wall's Drug Store in South Dakota? It is virtually nothing in the middle of nowhere, yet it has become a tourist attraction. Such a goal will take many years (if not decades) to achieve, but we must start to develop our marketable history—today.

Outsourcing is another problem closely associated with trade deficits. When so-called American companies go offshore to avoid paying our skilled laborers and the United States corporate taxes, they take money away from our domestic spending cycle. These corporations do not mind exploiting cheap labor in other lands as long as they can make more profit for themselves without regard to our common good. This is, once again, a sign of unbridled capitalism. If only (by adding special tariffs) we could ban such overseas operations from selling their products in the United States. Let them lose the American market and watch their sales and profits plummet.

Not only do these companies pay their foreign employees a lower wage, many of those employees are forced to work under conditions that are unhealthy and unsafe—for there are no rules or regulations to follow in many of those far-off lands. Let us call it like it is—off-shore companies are often engaged in a modern-day form of slavery. We can either retreat to those good old days of sweat-shops, child-labor violations, and unsafe working conditions in order to compete with poorer nations, or we can stand our ground and demand higher worldwide standards. Let us play by good rules and not give way to the dictates of others who are in it for the fast buck. Let us shun all unpatriotic companies.

In terms of our national deficit—full employment far outweighs the perceived fears associated with government spending. Granted—the government should be the employer of last resort in a robust economy. Unemployment benefits are a drain on the system in that the government receives little of value in return for that initial outlay of tax dollars. It should also be mentioned once again that unemployment creates shortfalls in the Social Security Fund, similar retirement funds, and the Medicare Fund, which are likewise adding to the financial problems of the future.

I hope the above comments have taken the bogeyman out of deficit spending. We should review the following facts:

1. The United States has always had a deficit, and yet we are the wealthiest nation in the world.

2. Putting off infrastructure projects hurts both present and future generations.

3. If our concern is for future generations, let us tackle environmental issues now.

4. Cutting taxes might stimulate an economy and reduce the deficit, but increased employment will achieve even more.

5. Increased taxation without additional spending could reduce the deficit.

6. We need to realize that the ever-growing national debt is stated in fiat dollars.

7. No other country is going to take over the United States of America because of our deficit.

8. Additional employment actually strengthens retirement trust

funds and Medicare, thus making them more solvent in the future—even if this were to mean putting people on the government payroll.

Inflation

While still on the subject of economics, let us take a moment and talk about inflation. It too has an impact on the deficit. Fifty years ago a modest ranch home cost approximately $18,000 and a new Ford sedan $2,000. Today the same house would sell for $180,000 and the car would cost $20,000. Today we have more homeowners than ever before. The overall automobile industry manufactures cars at an unprecedented rate. (Unfortunately, US manufacturers have lost a sizable share of the automobile market.) Somehow, we have managed to cope with this thing called inflation. Remember, with more people working, more people can afford homes and automobiles—thus offsetting the additional payroll costs of hiring more employees. As a people, we are able to cope with inflation, provided it is gradual in nature.

Unfortunately, inflation is often the by-product of greed. This is an area where each citizen plays an important role. In many ways we are just as bad as the bankers and other manipulators of money. We all want more. We all want more for less. We want annual pay increases. We want more perks and benefits. We want more profit. We want less taxation so we can have more money. It seems that we are never satisfied and content. It is this behavior that causes inflation, devalues our currency, increases the deficit, requires more taxation, and forces the government to become more active in managing the nation's economy. Little wonder economists can't agree—too much human nature is involved.

Inflation isn't all bad, especially for the rich. While it negatively affects those on a fixed income, which is somewhat offset by Cost Of Living

Allowance (COLAs), it is a boon for property owners and those who hold paper assets. These people double the value of their assets almost overnight without lifting a finger. Those still working can cope with a modest rate of inflation, since they receive ongoing pay increases.

The rate of inflation has a very dramatic negative effect on the growth of the deficit. The weaker the dollar, the higher the interest rate on borrowed money, thus increasing the overall deficit. We should therefore make every effort to control the rate of inflation—any growth must be gradual, giving time for adjustment. A rapid inflationary growth rate could destabilize the entire economic system. We must exercise restraint when wanting higher wages and larger returns on investments. As individuals we will benefit more in the long term if we concentrate on creating job opportunities for everyone, rather than receiving a higher return on our meager monetary investments.

There is one more vital factor involving our capitalistic economic system. This factor is an absolute necessity in a democracy. Most citizens readily recognize the superficial aspects of this factor yet fail to appreciate the long-term consequences if we fail to address this need. So let us begin by exploring our

Employment Needs

With no spending money—there is no capitalism! The more spending money citizens have, the better our economic system works. I am, therefore, emphasizing once again that employment is a key factor for economic growth. When the private sector cannot create enough employment opportunities, then what should we do? Wring our hands and worry? Who can we turn to? There is an old saying: "If you need a helping hand, look at the end of your wrist." "We the people" owe it to ourselves to find a solution by offering a helping hand to ourselves and our fellow citizens.

One of the best defenses against a rapidly growing deficit is full employment coupled with following the principles outlined in the domestic spending cycle. As a nation, we would be better off financially if we set long-term goals as a priority rather than turning a quick buck through some sort of an investment strategy. That is to say, we should place a higher value on earning a wage as opposed to receiving higher returns on investments. Actual work should trump all investments!

By plowing profits back into upgrading their businesses (always attempting to build a better mousetrap, which supports innovation and creativity), companies and corporations will achieve more in the long haul than declaring an outrageous dividend just to satisfy investors or line executive pockets.

Adam Smith's theory of capitalism inadequately covers the need for full employment in a large democratic society such as ours. If capitalism is to succeed in a democracy, much thought must be given to the needs of all people to earn money. This income allows people to purchase products. It is these purchases that stimulate business and set in motion the capitalistic system. Adam's theory was driven by the concept of supply and demand. Production was also a vital element of his theory. A person or company could produce the most desirable product known to humankind. Such a product could be produced quickly—enough to satisfy demand through mass production. All this would be to no avail if no one could afford the product. Capitalism cannot succeed in a democracy if no one is working and/or earning spending money.

Employment represents the ignition switch in capitalism. It fires up the economic engine. FDR understood this principle. He poured money (fuel) into the hands of people. They spent that money purchasing products, and the engine began to sputter. He enriched the process with more work projects and more money—soon the engine began to hum. (Don't you just love metaphors?)

If there are large numbers of people without income, how could they enjoy capitalism? Without income, such citizens would be faced with famine or the need for charity, or the government would be required to become involved in their plight.

As we grow older, nearing that inescapable event called death, no longer able to produce something of value, having never acquired a nest egg, how would we then survive? We must ask ourselves: To whom could we turn in such a situation? Are we expected to pass silently into the night? Should we be handled like small children—to be seen and not heard?

While charity can be a blessing for both the giver and the receiver, people with pride would rather earn their own way through life. All they require is the opportunity to earn. So let us create employment opportunities for our fellow citizens. This can be accomplished by both business and government hiring employees. If the population outgrows the need for employment in the private sector, then the government must step in to fill that void.

Try to envision the long-term consequence of massive unemployment and the effect this will have on future safety nets. No employment equates to inadequate contributions to current safety net programs. No safety nets, or inadequate safety nets, will result in more senior suffering in the future.

Large businesses hire employees by the thousands while small businesses hire by ones and twos. Individual small businesses, when combined with other small businesses, hire more employees than do the collective giant corporations. Individually, they lack strength, but collectively they represent the backbone of our economic system. The Small Business Administration was created to help smaller employers.

While small entrepreneurs play a crucial role in capitalism, their individual smallness cannot rapidly change the course of a major economic downturn. Only large corporations and/or the government can make dramatic changes in the national unemployment rate. A normal economic recovery requires a great deal of consumer confidence, which slowly encourages small entrepreneurs with limited resources to hire additional employees—one by one. The deeper the recession, the more difficult and prolonged is the recovery process. It is for this reason that the current recovery is leaping ahead by centimeters. A cooperating and involved government could have ended this recession much sooner. Party politics is holding up the recovery process. It is not the fault of any one party but rather the fault of individual desires to dominate others. Elected officials must abandon party politics by not voting in blocks but rather voting based on the merits of the issues.

In order to jump-start an economy (on a nationwide basis), government involvement is required. This is against the current principles of fiscal conservative thinking. Such thinking is based upon fear of increasing the deficit, or perhaps increasing taxes, or too much government involvement in the lives of the people. The reader must look at these fears to determine their validity. Please keep in mind—the more employed citizens, the greater tax revenue for government. The more employed citizens, the stronger the retirement and Medicare funds. The more employed citizens, the less drain on entitlement programs. These are true deficit busters!

In a caring democracy, allowing famine to exist should never be a consideration. When using taxes to employ citizens, the government should expect to receive something of value in return. Improving highways with tax money benefits everyone, as opposed to providing unemployment benefits and receiving little in return. Receiving something of value from tax dollars makes taxation a good investment. Passing out food stamps could be a never-ending exercise leading to abuse of our tax system. The food-stamp program primarily benefits the recipient and fails to solve a problem in the long term.

There are many skeptics and many a naysayer in our midst. There are those who believe that welfare recipients are lazy freeloaders and the bane of our society. They have heard of some welfare queen who lives like royalty off the welfare system. Yes, such things happen! This is another application of my 2 percent theory. There are a few who will abuse the system, but 98 percent of the recipients need, and are worthy of, assistance. We cannot turn our backs on the truly needy because of the slimy few. We would need more law enforcement officers to police the system in order to control every possible abuse.

Infrastructure improvements go beyond construction activities. There is a tendency to overlook the human element associated with infrastructure needs. If we build more electrical grids, would we not need more electricians and engineers to service them? If we build more schools, would we not need more teachers to fill the classrooms?

National defense is the major obligation of our federal government. Securing our borders with fencing, well-spaced military outposts, electronic tracking devices, drones, etc., as well as beefing up our Coast Guard, would afford us a greater sense of security while creating much-needed employment opportunities.

Without war, the need for an extremely large standing army becomes unnecessary. Our army should be used more like a militia, as suggested in the Constitution. It should be kept within the borders of our country and used primarily for the defense of our homeland. We currently reimburse foreign governments for the use of overseas bases—another drain on our resources.

If we simply draw down the size of our army, we would create more unemployment without having an alternate plan of action. Here are a few possibilities for consideration: Keep the military personnel in uniform. Construct relatively small military garrison-type outposts (no more than two hundred miles apart) along the entire length of both land borders. Border patrol agents would be used only at official crossings dealing with legal matters. Army personnel would simply round up persons attempting to enter the country illegally and turn them over to the legally trained border patrol agents for screening and possible deportation.

Many would agree that exposure to military training often turns children into adults. Such training should be universal and mandatory, but only for a short-term duration (such as a six-month boot camp). This modern-day militia would learn how to handle emergency situations such as disaster relief, fighting wildfires, mob control, flood control, and assisting in search and rescue missions. Experiencing the discipline of military life will help both males and females become better citizens. We would thus develop a reserve—a backup contingency plan designed to handle severe unforeseen emergency situations. Being a member of the militia was mandatory during our frontier period. It should be a civic duty borne by all citizens.

For our homeland defense and the protection of our interests abroad, we will require a large voluntary navy and air force. The navy and coast guard could be combined for economic purposes. The marines make outstanding guards for our worldwide embassies and military outposts. The marines should be the major military force stationed on foreign soil—their main assignment would be to guard and defend our interests and property (embassies) overseas.

The way in which we work has changed dramatically over the years. I remember as a young boy seeing over one hundred men, with their shirts off, sweating in the hot sun, laying railroad track. Today, that same work is done with a single machine and eight men. Back then, trains had crews—today, the engineer sits alone in the cab, and there is no caboose. With each passing year, we become more technologically advanced, thus requiring less physical effort and fewer people to do the same type of work. Soon there will be too few buttons to push and too many unemployed fingers to do the pushing. There is nothing wrong with making work easier. The trick will be to make more work available. Again, there are numerous ways to produce employment opportunities if we are willing to modify our thinking. European countries with very high unemployment ratios would do well to follow some of the approaches mentioned in this book.

Sufficient employment, coupled with taxation, provides a sound system for the disabled, orphaned, and elderly. Employment of a large working middle class is the solution for maintaining our democracy.

Employment, regardless of whether people are working for the government or in the private sector, helps to control the deficit and enhances the spirit of capitalism. Private sector employment is more desirable, but government employment is not without merit when looking at the big picture. Government must provide these safeguards when the private sector cannot.

Another way to increase employment for US citizens is to remove all illegal aliens from within our borders. This is an issue that many elected officials are reluctant to address. We can appreciate the desire of those individual illegal aliens to remain in our country. We can understand that deportation will create problems for certain families; however, humanitarian issues could be handled on a case-by-case basis while identifying and removing those with no justifiable reason for remaining in our country.

If need be, temporary work permits to allow foreign workers to pick fruits and vegetables could be established. At the end of the harvest season the permits would expire, and the aliens would be required to leave the country. A fair wage could be a matter of contract. Working under such a contract could be tax-free and without rights to future benefits. Only actual workers—not their families—would be allowed into our country during the harvest season. They should be required to carry suitable health care insurance while in the United States.

Illegal aliens work cheaply and are often paid under the table, thus avoiding the payment of any form of taxation. Employers should be required to pay their share of taxes. If this cheap labor source (which includes housekeepers, maids, nannies, and landscape technicians) were to disappear, many of our legal citizens would have to be hired. Hiring companies might be required to raise prices for their products or go out of business. If they produce a worthwhile product, they should be able to raise their prices, as would all their competitors. If that were the case, we, the consumer, would pay a few pennies more for their products. We would recover from this financial loss by not having our own taxes raised, because there would be fewer social needs.

When an employer hires someone off the street, he or she does so without regard for many human-rights principles. They are looking for cheap labor in order to save a few dollars. These so-called benevolent employers avoid paying payroll taxes, which in turn deprives the government—and the many programs sponsored by government—of revenue. They in fact are cheating each and every law-abiding, tax-paying citizen. Such people are not paying their fair share of taxes. Let us call it like it is—these are cheapskates and tax-dodgers who call themselves Americans.

If the current law were enforced, more of our fellow citizens would have jobs that paid a living wage, thus enabling them to come off the unemployment rolls. They would pay their fare share of taxes, thereby enhancing the financial stability of such programs as Social Security. By coming off the unemployment rolls and paying their share of income taxes, the deficit would be decreased. We would, in theory, have less tax to pay if everyone paid his or her fair share of taxes. In short, we would pay more for our cut-up chicken and less in taxes. It might become a matter of more inflation versus less deficit and taxation. We will never know the overall value of this proposal without trying to incorporate it into our economic system. Our current liberal approach to immigration is anti–deficit reduction. Our immigration policy should not be based on alluring ethnic groups into one political party or the other.

We run a terrible security risk by not knowing who is in our country. It is said that we have over eleven million illegal and unidentified aliens in our country. That figure might not include the harder-to-identify illegal aliens who have crossed over our northern border. (For those with short memories: Remember the bomber who crossed over from Canada to Port Angeles, Washington? He was on his way to bomb the Los Angeles International Airport when apprehended.) A porous border is an open border.

During a required sorting-out process, all illegal aliens would have to be properly identified. Next to securing our borders, the identification of all people living within our borders is extremely important for our security. This might require all adults (including we who are of colonial heritage) to carry a national identity card—not unlike a driver's license. (Here come the fear mongers!) God-fearing, law-abiding citizens would have nothing to fear but fear itself. If you have something to hide, then of course you would tremble at this thought. If all children were registered, it might help put many pedophiles and would-be kidnappers out of business. Be realistic—what more could our government do to any of us with or without an identity card? A law-abiding citizen does not drive a car without his or her driver's license.

During any sorting-out process, more federal immigration officers could be employed to enforce the rules (thereby creating more job opportunities for our current citizens). Such government employment would pay for itself in terms of reducing the deficit in numerous ways.

Employers who hire illegal aliens should be fined according to established law. The fines should make profiteering on the backs of what can only be described as slave labor, unprofitable. Again, more officers would be needed to enforce the program (creating even more job opportunities for our citizens).

So there we have it! These suggestions would create thousands of jobs, and our capitalistic economic system would still be intact. We would be making saner use of our military while cutting back on deficit spending. We would make our borders more secure while increasing employment opportunities for our citizens. We would improve our infrastructure for the benefit of all citizens. We would get more people to pay their fair share of taxes, thereby reducing the need to raise other taxes even further. These are win-win suggestions which, unfortunately, will not line the pockets of corrupt officials and therefore have little chance of becoming a reality. "We the people" must push for such changes, or they will never happen.

No attempt to explain or justify the way in which financial institutions handle investments or other monetary affairs has been made in this book. As little people we have nothing to offer the global financial manipulators. What they can do to us is beyond our control and understanding. Many of these financial giants, more than likely, have never done an honest day's work in their lives. Many survive by cutting corners, bending rules, and often scamming their way through life. Like parasites, they live off the true physical efforts of working men and women. These unfortunate realities are at the root of the "Occupy Wall Street" movement.

They say money talks. A lot of money not only talks—it screams! Our focus shall now turn to collective individualism—the forerunner of lobbying. After which, we will begin discussing a wide variety of issues relative to our present-day concerns.

Collective Individualism

The concept of collective individualism in America dates back to the early 1800s during the lifetime of Thomas Jefferson. Jefferson believed strongly in the principle of the individual vote. Each citizen was to be represented by an elected member of Congress. It would be difficult to find any citizen opposed to such a basic concept.

The problem appears to have begun shortly after Jefferson left office. An orator and statesman named Daniel Webster approached Congress on behalf of a union over a common problem that needed to be addressed. Webster was, in fact, speaking on behalf of this group and not for any one individual. The concept of collective individualism is said to have had its beginning in the New World around that time.

The Supreme Court reviewed the legality of this issue and overrode Jefferson's objections. In siding with Webster in this matter, the Court allowed the concept of collective individualism to exist.

We must now give some thought to that early Court decision—for it will usher in the practices of lobbying Congress and collective bargaining. There are both good and bad points to these practices. Many citizens belong to organizations that do both, such as unions, shareholder groups, corporations, and the ever-growing AARP. Members of such groups donate to Political Action Committee (PAC) funds that are designed to petition Congress through lobbying. More than likely, no one on that bygone Supreme Court would have been able to foretell the future consequences of their position.

Many believe that lobbying leads to a form of bribery that represents a flaw in our system of government. Should we do away with the ability of groups to present their problems before Congress? Perhaps group leaders could testify before Congressional committees but not be allowed to solicit support from individual members or political parties. If we could somehow remove money and various other perks from the equation, we would have a government more in tune with individual needs.

Shall we all hold our breath and wait for that better day? The only way to keep money from talking is to do away with mouthpieces. Unfortunately, this impacts democracy! Any attempt on the part of government to control this situation will have to focus on the money part of the equation.

Congress has placed restrictions on political contributions, but loophole after loophole has been found to circumvent the intent of those restrictions. Many politicians need money to conduct reelection campaigns. To block money from poor candidates would allow only the rich and powerful to run for office. This is truly a Catch-22 situation. There is no simple way to curtail this form of bribery. Perhaps Congress could tax dollar-for-dollar donations given by Super PACs and apply that as taxable income toward the deficit. In short, you could buy a politician if you pay a sales tax!

The final solution may depend upon the intelligence of voters. A well-informed public can discern between fact and fiction—between lies and half truths. It will become necessary for government and large corporations to become as transparent as possible in all their decision-making processes in order to establish trust. Sunshine laws for all segments of society should be established and enforced. Such openness might force those in power to be more honest. Sunshine laws within all government agencies would downplay fears of "big government" taking away some of our freedoms. The Freedom of Information Act was aimed in the right direction and has brought to light many questionable governmental practices. Perhaps something similar is needed for the private sector. To avoid future economic accidents, private corporations should "turn on their lights" (as a safety precaution) in order for us to see what's coming down the pike.

As a side issue—now enters another political sleaze factor: the Constitution contains the basic instructions for determining the number of voters required per member of the House of Representatives. Each state is allowed to draw up the boundary lines for its allowable Congressional Districts. Gerrymandering is the name given to the act of drawing boundaries primarily along political party lines. Such action places membership in a political party ahead of all other considerations. It creates safe districts for certain representatives. In such districts, there may as well be only one political party. In the eyes of many citizens, this safety net for politicians is unwarranted. Some refer to it as "stacking the deck." This practice detracts from the nobility of the vote. Let us do away with safe districting for political reasons and make every politician work for his or her job.

The following are thoughts and opinions presented for discussion and consideration. Readers need not agree with any of this and perhaps have thoughts and opinions of their own on these and similar subjects. Through discussion we often learn the views of others. We see the other side of the coin. It is the first step toward achieving any form of consensus. So let us begin by assessing:

Our Role in the World

Can a world power be an isolationist country? That almost sounds like an oxymoron! Can we be a generous nation and still put our own country first? Of course, a great nation can do many things, but one cannot be everything to everybody. Militarily, we cannot be the policeman for the entire world. As humanitarians, we are not capable of feeding the entire world. There are limitations to our ability to help others. In this segment, we shall explore ways to assist others while, at the same time, benefiting our own country. In so doing, we will be capable of providing even more assistance to others in the future.

In a real sense, doctors and nurses must be physically able to render care before they can help others. As a nation, we must remain healthy in order to assist others. From a realistic viewpoint we must say, "US First!"

Currently, we provide subsidies to some farmers for not growing crops. In fact, we are paying them to do nothing or to increase their income. How uncapitalistic can this be? We taxpayers should be getting something in return for those subsidies. In many places around the world there are food shortages, especially during times of disaster. Large amounts of food are required to sustain life in such stricken areas. Could we combine our nonproductive and price-supporting farm subsidies with our humanitarian relief efforts?

We could pay farmers to grow winter wheat (excellent for long-term storage). Wheat is the manna of life—every culture knows how to make it eatable, and it contains no religious taboos. Then let us build and/or fill government storage facilities (silos, etc.) with this wheat. This wheat would not appear on the open market but would rather be held in reserve for disaster relief. Examples of this type of government involvement can be found in many Old Testament stories such as Genesis 39–41.

This wheat could then be transported via American-owned ships and planes to the needy around the world. Each bag would contain words and symbols indicating that these were gifts from the people of the United States. (This action is designed to promote goodwill for our country while at the same time helping others.) It appears we would benefit more by sharing our abundance, rather than giving away less essential items.

If we feel more inclined to promote subsidies, then perhaps our government could purchase much-needed pharmaceuticals from drug companies to be used in Third World countries. This is not unlike some farm subsidies in that it involves a form of price controls. The government purchases new, expensive drugs at a high cost in exchange for those companies charging less to our citizens. In reality the government would be subsidizing pharmaceutical research. This research is designed to make life better for all of us and thus serves the common good. These new wonder drugs would be transported by American companies and clearly marked as coming from the people of the United States, as stated earlier.

In manufacturing states with high unemployment, the government could purchase water purification trucks, tanks, and equipment for countries in need of pure or cleaner water. Once again, these items are shipped by American companies and bear our logo. Many countries need good water, and we have the technical ability to produce it. This creates work where work is most needed here at home while also helping others.

A few more fully equipped hospital ships could be built by our government and stationed around the world to address the medical needs of Third World countries. These mobile hospitals, with multiple helicopter pads, would be manned by naval personnel. The government would pay the medical school costs for individual doctors, dentists, technicians, and nurses in exchange for some years of service aboard these ships. This is not unlike agreements offered to cadets graduating from military schools such as Annapolis, West Point, and the Air Force Academy. One would hope that this would encourage more young citizens to join the medical profession, since there will never be enough medical practitioners for our aging society. Perhaps service aboard such a ship could be applied toward their intern*ship* requirements.

Because of our technical ability and related advantages, we are capable of sharing technical assistance to underdeveloped nations. Sharing knowledge costs so little yet can enhance living conditions for the masses. The Peace Corps is an outstanding example of such ideals. Such programs should be encouraged and supported by our foreign service within the US Agency for International Development. Let us flood the world with volunteer teachers, for they will accomplish more than military might. It is hard to win the hearts and minds of people when your representatives carry weapons. Some nations may be backward, but they are not stupid. Most people are smart enough to smile and be agreeable in the presence of an armed soldier or policeman. How they truly feel about such foreign intruders is another matter. Such uncertainties do not exist when people are dealing with members of the Peace Corps. These unarmed citizens will more often be greeted with open arms in those far-off lands. Such efforts by good people could lead to peace on earth one day.

Many of the examples outlined above would promote goodwill toward our country while helping to minimize economic problems at home. We would be creating work opportunities in America, enhancing medical research for the betterment of all humankind, encouraging growth in the medical field, while helping those most in need of assistance. We would be receiving something in return for our generosity. Foreign aid should never be in the form of money. Money often finds its way into the pockets of the greedy and not the needy. Money never buys loyalty!

Military weapons assistance often comes back to haunt us. We furnish weapons to one faction during a conflict only to find those same weapons being used against us in a later conflict. Let us allow other countries to duke out their own problems without our taking sides. We should exercise restraint before becoming involved in the problems of other nations. If it becomes absolutely necessary to confront another nation, we should do so only with the approval of the vast majority of the members of the United Nations. No longer should we become engaged in foreign land wars. Bombings, missile attacks, and covert actions (including assassinations), after a fair warning, should be the extent of our involvement against radical individuals, nations, or groups.

There are many issues in which all the countries of the world have a stake. The United Nations provides a forum for discussing such problems. Global warming, the greenhouse effect, the ozone layer, rain forests, etc., require a response by the family of nations. America acting alone could never solve global issues. Without worldwide support, we might just as well throw up our hands and surrender to the inevitable.

As American capitalists, there is nothing wrong with suggestions such as those mentioned above. We will still be a democratic republic. We will still be a major player on the world stage. We can show that we have both a heart and a mind when dealing with world problems. The spirit of cooperation between nations must be developed to the highest degree possible if our ultimate aim is to achieve peace on earth and good will toward men. We sing about this concept every December and only mouth the words the rest of the year.

Environmental Issues

As I have previously stated, environmental issues should be of more concern than deficit spending. The deficit can ultimately be handled in several ways, and people will survive. There is no substitution for running out of clean air and pure water. When such a resource is depleted—that's it! This is our planet, and so far there is nowhere we can go if we make it uninhabitable. Human kind must exercise good stewardship over God-given gifts or face drastic negative consequences.

There are many citizens who worry over the extinction of whales, seals, spotted owls, etc. This is not to detract from those concerns but rather to focus on human needs. We know the surface of the earth has undergone change over the millennia and will continue to do so.

We realize the ice glaciers are receding at a rapid rate. Many claim our atmosphere is warming.

The surface of the globe is primarily covered with water, yet most of it is undrinkable. We use available (and some non-restorable) resources to heat our homes and fuel our automobiles. So what must we do to ensure the survival of our species in the future?

Let us begin by prioritizing human needs. At the top of the list should be our need for drinking water. There are many places on this planet currently in need of water. The underground water table is slowly diminishing. In the years to come, more and more people will be living on this planet, and they will require good water in order to survive. So let us begin by tackling the upcoming water-shortage crisis while we can—before it is truly a crisis. Let us be proactive and prepare for the future. The following thoughts are geared toward enhancing our infrastructure and addressing current employment needs while at the same time considering the well-being of future generations.

Our economic system (capitalism) prevents the private sector from tackling this problem. Currently there is no profit incentive for producing more water. No bottom line—no interest! Once the demand outweighs the supply, the vultures will smell the dying corpses and come to the rescue. No one should expect proactive planning from the private sector in this regard. By the time the private sector goes into action, tens of thousands will already have suffered. Is that what we need or want?

Our nation is blessed in that we are surrounded by water, albeit salt water. The greatest percentage of our population lives close to those saltwater shores. Some of those areas, from time to time, experience drought conditions. Let us begin by providing more drinking water for that heavy concentration of people, especially along the coast of Southern California and the warm Gulf state of Texas.

Here is a suggestion that can be modified to address this problem. Because of the existing earthquake possibilities under California and off its coast, and the devastation that could be brought about by hurricanes in the Gulf of Mexico, this suggestion contains a measure of mobility. It also provides a measure of flexibility designed to help during temporary drought conditions anywhere around our shoreline.

The government could build several large (aircraft-carrier-size) ships in our existing shipyards, creating employment in those areas. In lieu of hangar decks, flight decks, and heavy armament, the ships would be fully equipped with desalinization equipment. A land-based pipeline could then be connected to the ship and desalinized water pumped into nearby man-made reservoirs or storage tanks. The pipeline could be disconnected and capped in the event of an approaching storm and the ship moved to a safer location. In the event of an earthquake, the ship, not being a fixed structure, could better ride out the ground movement. (The alternative would be, of course, stationary desalinization plants.) There would be many details to work out, but any problems encountered would be within humankind's capability to solve. Mobility simply enhances flexibility!

The government could contract with companies in the heavily unemployed industrial states to build the desalinization equipment, which then can be transported to the ships and installed. This would create work where work is needed.

Thus far, we have created work, provided transportation, and enhanced the future in the name of the common good. What will the inland states gain from all this? Under current water right laws, states are required to allow a certain amount of river water to pass beyond their boundaries. (In short, Colorado cannot keep all of the Colorado River's water for itself. It must allow water to pass downstream. The amount of such water is a matter of current regulation.)

If the coastal areas had sufficient water, the interior states could keep more inland water for themselves by simply changing the water right laws. This would allow more water for agricultural needs in the breadbasket states. This is just one of many ways to improve the future for our children and grandchildren.

As for the ships or plants—once completed and in place, they would be turned over to some local authority for administration, upkeep, and repair. This is similar to the way the Golden Gate Bridge is operated. When needed and after being placed on line, a user fee might be required to defer expenses—this should prove to be cheaper than the current bottled water that is sold at a penny per ounce.

This project should begin slowly by designing one ship for testing purposes—and working out the bugs. As the more serious long-term problem approaches, we would be better able to address the needs of the people through mass production of such plants and facilities in relatively short order. Good planning and development takes time—we should begin that phase soon.

So much for water! Let us turn our thoughts to electricity. As individuals and as a nation, we are extremely dependent upon electricity for our everyday living needs. It seems as if all our modern gadgets require battery chargers. (At night my home is a sea of little red, amber, and green flickering lights.) Electricity is a clean source of energy when it finally reaches the home or office. Generating electricity can be either clean or dirty, depending on the fuel source. We have wind, solar, water, as well as coal to consider in connection with generating electricity.

We may eventually be forced to come to grips with using fossil fuels, such as coal, to run electricity-producing generators. We, as a nation, are blessed with an abundant supply of coal. It has been estimated that our coal supply could last for more than two hundred years. The problem is how to burn it without causing excessive pollution. The ability to solve this problem would make us one step closer toward requiring less imported fuels. Time and research will afford the answer someday. Government could become involved by funding research in this regard.

Our concern at present is with the electrical delivery system. Brownouts and blackouts are no longer acceptable conditions. Weather conditions can cause major problems. There is a security risk if terrorists could destroy a major portion of our current grid system. We must address these concerns first. We must devise a grid system impervious to attack and remove the possibilities for brownouts or blackouts. New electrical construction should be underground; and we should systematically replace all major overhead lines with underground lines, thus eliminating the majority of weather-related problems.

The American automobile industry might be well advised to design a class of electric cars primarily suited for use during rush hour in highlypopulated cities. They should be marketed as a rush-hour car, with virtually no frills, suitable for driving to and from work or school—small in size and easy to park. In many major cities parking is not only expensive; it is becoming difficult to find. Smaller cars would mean more parking spaces. The main point is to save on fuel (especially purchasing foreign fuel) while cleaning up the atmosphere.

The government could become a major player in reducing the need for foreign fuel imports, reducing pollution, making electric cars more affordable, and reducing the deficit. The federal government owns and operates a massive fleet of vehicles. Replacing each and every vehicle with an electric-powered car would: (1) stimulate the auto industry; (2) reduce pollution; (3) reduce fuel imports; and finally, (4) reduce the deficit. In this regard, let us take a look at the current US Postal Service.

As our demographics and technology have changed, the importance of having a postal service has diminished. We still have need for the postal service, but it does require a measure of modernization by replacing outdated concepts. The biggest drain on postal resources stems from the truly rural districts. I am not suggesting the layoff of personnel, which would be contraindicated at this time. Let us begin slowly in our aim toward making it a more productive service. All motorized rural routes should be reduced to three days per week (Monday, Wednesday, Friday for one route; Tuesday, Thursday, Saturday for another route). This action alone would cut fuel and vehicle maintenance costs by 50 percent in those rural areas. The human carriers would find work in their local post office sorting mail or assisting customers at the counter. The staff would be reduced gradually, under the principle of attrition. In this modern era, with e-mail, i-Pods, and unlimited usage of cell phones, the need for daily mail delivery has greatly diminished. There is a system in place for emergency mail—it goes by names such as Fed Ex or UPS. The delivery of junk mail could take a day or two longer, but for the majority, who cares?

Now let us turn our thoughts to more lofty issues. The government is involved in many social issues that have an impact on certain aspects of the Bill of Rights. When disagreements arise regarding the Bill of Rights, the government has little choice but to engage the issues. So let us jump into the fray and share our thoughts.

Religion and Government

Another demographic change that has come to pass over the years involves religion. The early settlers of our country were for the most part Christians of various denominations. Many people refer to the United States as a Christian nation. Christianity (when combining all 362 Christian denominations) is in fact the largest of all religions within our borders; however, there are now great numbers of other religious people living among us. We might become less divisive in our relationships with others if we referred to ourselves as a pluralistic society comprised of many different ethnic, racial, and religious peoples, rather than emphasizing our Christian heritage. Christians are admonished to love their neighbors as themselves, thus making any form of bigotry hypocrisy on their part.

Religion and good government are not enemies. It is not a case of one versus the other. Good government needs and desires good religions to strengthen the moral fiber of the nation. A democracy requires high standards from the citizens it serves. In contrast—Communism, as practiced in the former Soviet Union, had contempt for all things religious. It required fewer than seventy years for that system of government to fail. The history of Western religions makes for an interesting study regarding the development of mankind. The origin of Christianity is especially interesting, as it involved the unification of an imperial government in a bygone era.

Emperor Constantine the Great (AD 272–337), having trouble unifying his people, used religion to bring social order to his far-reaching empire. Claiming he had received a sign from God in the form of a cross, he converted to Christianity. He called together the first ecumenical council, to be held at Nicaea in AD 325. The Nicene Creed developed and Christianity became the official religion for Constantine's entire empire. (Just a few decades earlier, Christians were being fed to the lions at the Coliseum in Rome.) The Nicene Creed was the official beginning of the universal (Catholic) church. At the Synod of Carthage (AD 397), the current twenty-seven books of the New Testament were confirmed by those present and canonized as part of the Holy Bible, thereby uniting both the old and new testaments. This set the stage for dividing the calendar of time between BC (before Christ) and AD (Anno Domini—after the birth of our Lord).

At a later date, King Henry VIII of England, known for a while as the "Defender of the Faith," denounced the authority of the pope and created his own version of Christianity. Once again the world had a government-controlled religion called the Church of England. Those who failed to follow or accept the teachings of that church were persecuted. A reformation ensued and various denominations of Christianity sprang up overnight throughout Europe. The powerful Catholic Church seated in Rome (the Vatican having since become a state government unto itself) soon felt the effects of this schism.

A majority of our original thirteen colonies came into being as a result of humans seeking religious freedom. They came from the British Isles in an attempt to worship their God as they saw fit. Back in England, many suffered religious persecution because they could not accept the teachings of the national church. Each colony brought a devout Christian belief system to our shores. The Maryland Colony was established by Catholics. The Puritans landed at what is now called Plymouth, Massachusetts. The Quakers settled in Pennsylvania, Anglicans settled in Virginia and Unitarians in the New England states.

The New World was believed to be a land of promise—free of the religious bigotry that they had experienced in their native land. Our Founding Fathers were the beneficiaries of this newfound freedom and so gave expression to religious freedom in both the Declaration of Independence and our Constitution with its Bill of Rights.

In those early documents our Founding Fathers referred to "God" and the "Almighty" in a generic way but never mentioned a specific religion. The closest they came was in the closing sentence of the Constitution when they gave the then-current reference to the date: "in the year of our Lord." Was the fact that a specific God was not mentioned an oversight or was it an intentional omission? It appears that "the intent of Congress" was to allow us to be a pluralistic society. Call the "Creator of All" by any name or in any tongue and that spirit becomes the "Almighty God." If that Great Spirit created one of us, it created all of us. If you believe in a God, then you must accept the fact that we are all his (creation) children—which includes agnostics and atheists. So we must move beyond denominations and creeds! "To each his own" in the land of the free!

It is quite possible that the Founding Fathers were not thinking of Hindus, Moslems, Buddhists, or Jews during the revolutionary period. Perhaps their only concern was over the various branches within Christianity. It matters not, as the intent remains the same. The first Amendment to our Constitution reads: "Congress shall make no law respecting an establishment of religion, or prohibiting the free exercise thereof." If there is to be no law establishing religion, then those who do not want religion jammed down their throats should likewise have their rights protected—in short, atheists and agnostics also have rights in this regard. We should consider ourselves as belonging to a pluralistic society, as opposed to a Christian nation, if we desire the blessings associated with democracy. Religious freedom demands adherence to the principle of choice. The ability to choose is one of the definitions of freedom noted previously in this book.

In a democracy such as ours we must first and foremost protect the individual rights of our fellow citizens—and they are required to return the favor. We must protect each others' rights regardless of race, ethnic background, sex, or religious belief. If in fact we are living in a truly Christian country, the idea of tolerance, patience, love, and forgiveness should be acceptable to all members of that creed. Or are there some who are Christians in name only?

Within differing religions there will naturally be differing moral values and beliefs. One could argue endlessly over various religious differences with no agreement as to who is right and who is wrong. Arguing over religious doctrine is pointless, so let us learn to accept differences of opinion.

Unfortunately, there are a great number of our citizens who honestly believe our country is going to hell. They desire to return to the days of our Founding Fathers in order to recapture the liberty and freedoms they enjoyed. For them, we are moving further and further away from righteousness by tolerating such things as homosexuality; by not allowing prayer in schools; by not allowing religious icons to be displayed on government property. They have a never-ending list of grievances and concerns along such lines. Surely they have a right to their opinions in a democracy such as ours. Religious extremists must someday accept different ideologies and concentrate on the basic teachings of their faith—such as love and peace. Matters of faith can be so intense as to override any logical thought process. Some might refer to this as a display of bigotry. Yes, an overtly religious person can be a bigot!

The First Amendment to our Constitution basically requires government not to become involved in matters of religion. To ensure this separation between church and state, religions are exempt from taxation. In deference to this doctrine of separation—religious groups should refrain from imposing their denominational beliefs on others. What is good for the goose …!

There exists in the world today another form of government that is based upon religious doctrine. Such a government is called a theocracy. For many years such a government controlled the people of Afghanistan. This government is better known as the Taliban. The Taliban uses force and extremism to compel the people of Afghanistan to behave according to Taliban religious beliefs. The Taliban believe they hold the keys to religious truths and demand that everyone live up to those high standards. The Taliban did not start off using extreme punishment for alleged sinners. The onset was gradual, until a firm foothold was established within their community. Religious zeal often begins that way. A theocracy is an affront to the principles of a democracy—they cannot coexist.

In recent years, certain religious groups have attempted to interpret the Constitution in order to reflect their personal points of view. Some have gone so far as to seek legal interpretations of their beliefs through the court system, and therein lies a major problem.

Government should not be involved in ideological issues. We need government to govern on issues of state. Government should not be taking sides in purely religious matters. There are religious denominations that abhor birth control in any way shape or form. These groups are entitled to their opinions, but should they attempt to impose their position upon others? If a religious group objects to any form of birth control, let them begin by compelling members of their own faith to abide by such beliefs. One religion should not attempt to force members of other religions to accept its point of view, for to do so is an affront to democracy.

Did the US Supreme Court overstep its bounds when agreeing to hear Roe vs. Wade? They could have, and perhaps should have, refused to hear the case. One can easily reason that it would be next to impossible to determine the exact time, date, and place as to when conception occurs. An unenforceable law makes a mockery out of our judicial system. If conception is a key factor in determining what life is under the law, those taking the morning-after pill could perhaps one day be charged with premeditated murder. We must keep our government from going down such a slippery slope.

Section 1 of the Fourteenth Amendment states that in order to enjoy the rights guaranteed under our Constitution, a person must be a citizen either "born or naturalized." An unborn fetus would not be considered a citizen based upon this requirement. Conception does not equate to citizenship under that provision.

The beginning of life does not meet the test of US citizenship. Citizenship cannot begin before birth! This is the reason for that piece of paper called a "birth certificate." From a biological view—life does begin at conception. From a purely legal view—life begins with birth. We are not a nation of biologists. Our nation is a nation built upon the principles of law.

Between conception and the actual birth of a child many situations can develop. There are miscarriages—both natural and self-induced. There are stillborn births at various stages of development. There are premature births where babies of limited weight cannot survive. Is a stillbirth God's way of aborting life? Are all abortions of life sinful in the eyes of God? Who speaks for God and under what authority?

Asking nine mere mortals, the justices of the US Supreme Court, to determine God's intent places a tremendous burden upon their shoulders—well beyond their pay grade. They must limit their rulings to points of law as applied to the Constitution. The Congress cannot make any law regarding religion. The Supreme Court should not be making laws, only interpreting the law. Unfortunately, this can of worms has been opened.

In their landmark 1973 decision, the Supreme Court attempted to consider both sides in their ruling. They divided human pregnancies into three trimesters with the right-to-life position becoming stronger as the pregnancy ran its course. Abortion upon demand (choice) is to be allowed during the first trimester. There are many conditions and restrictions applied to abortions during the second trimester. There must be extraordinary circumstances that would allow an abortion during the third and final trimester. While in the eyes of many this might not be a perfect ruling, it shows that a great deal of thoughtful deliberation was given to this subject. The nine justices, short on heavenly direction, administered human laws in a down-to-earth manner. The Roe vs. Wade decision was a Solomon-like ruling (cutting the gestation period into thirds), and still it is not to the liking of many.

Can those who disagree with that decision still march in protest? Of course they can! It would be far better if they marched for life rather than against abortions. Marching *for* something rather than marching *against* something is far less confrontational and mean-spirited. Such an approach to delicate issues proves we can disagree and still be civil!

More recently, the issue of same-sex marriages has come to our national attention. The state of California held an election referendum where citizens were asked to vote on the proper definition of marriage (*Webster's* dictionary lists five definitions). A majority of those voting (shame on those who did not vote) decided that marriage should be between one man and one woman. This would take away the rights of anyone who might feel differently—such as those desiring to live in a homosexual relationship. The result of that election has been challenged and will more than likely be heard someday by the US Supreme Court.

The issue was originally placed on the ballot by individuals who were not actually voting *for* someone but rather voting *against* someone. Married couples already enjoyed all the rights of marriage, so this new political referendum did nothing to affect their standing within the community. The purpose of this referendum was to keep couples within the homosexual community from having the same rights and privileges enjoyed by heterosexual couples. A better way to have handled this difference would have been to create, recognize, and legalize "personal partnership agreements" rather than squabbling over the definition of marriage. As of this writing, two levels of the California court system have heard arguments and ruled in favor of striking down the results of that earlier referendum. More appeals will surely follow. This is a good example of a majority vote challenging the rights of a minority—

illustrating the difference between a republic and a democracy as pointed out in part 1 of this book.

The issue of citizens not being allowed to serve in any branch of our armed forces because of their sexual orientation has been recently put to rest by a presidential Executive Order. The former "Don't Ask, Don't Tell" policy, affecting military personnel, has since been rescinded, thus ending another example of discrimination within our country. Sex should be the last thing on the minds of service personnel during the course of battle—be they gay or straight. The willingness to die for one's country should be the ultimate test of a worthy American.

While a good measure of morality is needed within government, as much, if not more, is needed in the private sector. The priests, ministers, rabbis, and clergy of all religions should preach and teach their denominational beliefs to their flocks from their pulpits and classrooms. They should be teaching each member the difference between right and wrong and, one hopes, encouraging them to make good choices. The concept of choice has been with us from the very beginning of recorded history.

For those who believe in the Bible, as recorded in the book of Genesis, Adam and Eve were given a choice. As recorded, they were commanded not to eat of a forbidden fruit for, if they did, they would have to suffer the consequences. Many believe they made the wrong choice. Others believe they made the right choice—either way, choice was at the core (apple or otherwise) of that story.

The ability to make decisions is one of God's greatest gifts to mankind. If God wanted mankind to do the *goose-step*—surely he would have made line dancing the eleventh commandment.

Many parents resent school involvement in the subject of sex education. Granted, family values and sex education can be taught by good parents, but who teaches those children who do not belong to a complete and wholesome family? It is for this reason that schools became involved in sex education. This is a reality—not a product of wishful thinking or religious ideology. Teaching good family values is an appropriate function of good parenting.

That statement begs the following question: "Who teaches children about sexuality if they are involved in an incestuous family relationship?" It is easy to see why some parents would rather not have the schools involved. Recent studies have shown that sexual abuse of children by members of the immediate family is extremely common and on the rise. Good parents will teach properly, and the schools will reinforce a major portion of those teachings. Parents might concentrate more on the spiritual relevancy of sex, allowing the schools to comment on the physical side of sex. Teaching hygiene (communicable disease control) and the avoidance of premature births has a place within our society through public education.

In summarizing this segment, we should think for ourselves. If one dislikes big, intrusive government, here is a good starting point. Don't allow government to be involved in religious issues. Here is the best part: if politicians did not talk about moral issues, their debate time would be cut in half—giving their tongues and our ears a much-needed rest. Having politicians debate moral issues can often be both pathetic and laughable.

We will now switch from discussing teaching moral issues to talking about public school teachings.

Education in America

As we continue discussing changing demographics, we must include formal education in our public school systems throughout the United States. In the minds of many people, each state or local authority should be responsible for its own school system. Why, then, is the federal government involved in educational activities? We will attempt to address that question within this segment.

Year after year, the subject of education in America becomes part of the political conversation. We are told that our school system, in many ways, is substandard compared with school systems throughout the industrial world. We have fallen behind other nations in teaching mathematics and sciences.

If we are to compare our educational system with other industrial nations, we should consider the underlying difference in concepts. In the United States, we place a greater value on a well-rounded education system. In much of Europe, they approach life through specialization. They produce more eggheads than the United States does.

We must remember that Europe is the home of the "guild system" that began with medieval trade associations. Young boys, at an early age, became apprentices within a given trade—usually following in their fathers' footsteps. In current-day England, at age eleven a child is given a test that determines whether he or she will go to a trade school or continue with more academic studies. Those who continue in academia take tests for advancement in specialized studies. By the time they reach the university level, they are ready to work on their elected major. Most American children enter college without the slightest idea as to what they wish to do with the rest of their lives. More than likely this uncertainty is encouraged by the desire for our children to be more educationally well rounded. "Jack-of-all-trades and master of none" is an appropriate description of many Americans.

Here is another difference: in many industrial nations, the school day is longer, and the summer vacation period, shorter. Europeans regard schooling as a job. A more formal relationship exists between student and teacher. Perhaps we should consider paying teachers more and adding to the hours they work. Perhaps if students and teachers wore uniforms, formality would be enhanced.

The American system evolved differently. In frontier times, small communities often hired a literate person to teach their children. The community furnished a one-room schoolhouse with living quarters in the rear for the teacher. Children of various ages sat in the same classroom, and the teacher taught different subjects to various groups of students. They shared desks, books, paper, and pencils. The children learned the basics for reading and writing, while the teacher earned a living.

Since those days, things have changed, especially in larger towns and cities. Now, each age group has a separate classroom. One subject is taught at a time. Each teacher has more children to contend with.

Much of what takes place in today's schoolrooms is similar to the methods used for decades, yet so much has changed within our society over those years. We now have more single-parent families and families where both parents work full-time than ever before. Such households have less time for teaching their children. These parents are struggling just to keep out of debt during difficult financial times. They go to work in the morning and return home at 5:00 p.m. or later. They prepare the evening meal, clean up, bathe, and prepare for the next day before going to bed, exhausted. Little time is allowed for sitting down with the children in order to furnish meaningful teaching lessons or review homework assignments. The children of these families leave school by 3:00 p.m. and go home to empty houses. They are referred to as "latchkey children." Yes, they have time for homework—they also have time for trouble during these unsupervised periods. They are faced with numerous distractions. Pleasure-seeking calls them away from a more productive course of action. Kids will be kids!

Local property taxes and special issues of municipal bonds are designed to promote and support schools and libraries—why involve the federal government? How can the government in far-off Washington, DC, know what is best for the children in New Mexico? Such concerns are expressed daily by those who oppose a big, intrusive federal government, especially as it applies to education.

Many parents are so disgusted with local school systems that they have turned to home teaching as an alternative. They have returned to the major principles associated with tutoring. This should be a wake-up call for those responsible for educating children. Local superintendents of schools, along with various principals and teacher unions, need to put their own desires aside and focus on the needs of the children. Tenure should be replaced by ability, if teaching is to remain an honorable profession. In many large metropolitan areas, teachers with seniority are allowed to select the best schools, in the best neighborhoods, and with the best behaved children rather than teach where their experience is most needed—in the ghetto or barrio.

An older teacher with years of experience might one day be unable to cope with rowdy teenagers. Ability, not tenure, should be a primary factor in maintaining employment as a teacher. Teachers who have trouble controlling a classroom full of lively children might be better at tutoring smaller groups in need of personal attention.

It is now time for another reality check. Not all states are equal in economic terms. In states where income is low, taxes are low. School buildings and equipment in the economically stressed states are obsolete by modern-day standards. The teachers' salaries are low, and the teachers' teaching credentials are below standard in many instances. The children in those states have less in the way of learning opportunities. Poverty prevails under these conditions. How can a poor state pull itself up by its bootstraps when it doesn't even have shoes?

The gap between those less fortunate states and the richer states has increased over the decades. As an economic class system among the states develops, the spirit of equality diminishes. Young adults with an inferior high school education will find it more difficult to obtain employment outside their local communities, for they have nothing to offer in a more sophisticated society. Noticeable educational differences will weaken our democracy! We should attempt to strengthen the weakest in order to achieve equality though government. If the reader disagrees, what would be a creative alternative? Is the status quo a solution?

Setting standards can be applied at local, state, and federal levels. This is normally achieved by testing the students. What is considered acceptable at the local level might be considered inferior at the state level. Should the state attempt to elevate the lower standard set by a local Board of Education? Or should the "anything goes" mentality of a local government prevail? Now apply this same principle to the various states versus the federal government. If setting minimum, yet acceptable, standards nationwide is considered a good idea, then chalk up another one for the federal government. If not, what would be a good alternative?

We are currently paying the price for years of segregation in the Southern states. Poverty runs rampant in many parts of Appalachia. We are aware of the special educational problems faced by Native Americans in the Southwest. The children of the "hoods" in larger cities require more hands-on attention. We can ignore such problems or we can try to rectify them. Many situations cross state lines and may therefore involve the federal government. Why haven't the state governments addressed these problems? How long should this neglect be allowed to continue?

Currently, federal taxes from more prosperous states are used to shore up the educational needs of less prosperous states. Is such action fair, warranted, and Constitutional? Is it in keeping with the principles of a democracy, which stresses equality? Or perhaps the uneducated in some states should be kept "barefoot and pregnant," as the saying goes.

If the federal government does not become involved in education, should it be left up to the various states? What would be the ultimate outcome? Will the neglected children suffer? Will ignorance breed more ignorance? The government (we the people) needs more, not fewer, educated people in order to compete with the rest of humankind.

Federal government involvement in education requires a host of rules, regulations, and restrictions (perhaps this is a modern version of the three Rs). If a state accepts federal funding, it must comply with many federal standards and requirements. States are not given federal funding with no strings attached. The amount of federal tax money given to a school district depends not only on the number of students in the state but on their attendance—this forces school districts to look into the problems associated with absenteeism. A student not in school will be educated on the streets—with frightening consequences.

If poor Mississippi needs money for education, then the federal government has every right to expect good results in return for its investment in the Mississippi school system. Mississippi cannot expect something for nothing! This method of redistribution of taxation is not going to change our form of government into socialism—in fact, it strengthens the concept of democracy by providing equality. Can Mississippi refuse to accept federal support? Yes, and suffer the consequences!

Teaching should be looked upon as an honorable profession. In days of yore, only the children of the wealthy received a formal education. Then, tutors were employed to teach these young minds. The tutor was also a mentor who taught a wide variety of subjects. The children received one-on-one instruction from someone who was almost a member of the family. Today, the children are herded from grade to grade, from subject to subject, from teacher to teacher. No longer is the teacher a mentor! No longer is there a close personal relationship between student and teacher. It appears we have missed the main element required for good teaching—a sound teacher-student relationship. Perhaps we cannot fully return to that bygone era because of economic restrictions, but maybe there is a way to bridge the gap to some degree.

Children are very capable of learning a great deal during the most formative school years—first, second, and third grades. At those ages, children face the least amount of peer pressure. This is a good time to introduce uniforms and dress codes—to instill a sense of belonging, of being part of a group. This is the time to develop penmanship, enhance reading and basic mathematical skills. Class size should never exceed twenty students (the smaller the better). We should utilize more teachers during these early years in order to make certain no student is left behind at the starting gate.

If there is a problem with language, those children who cannot speak English should be placed in a special first grade and taught nothing but English for one full year, regardless of the student's age. Anyone who cannot communicate properly will have a hard time fitting into society.

This is the time when a personal relationship is needed between student and teacher. Having the same teacher for the first three years of schooling may eliminate many social problems. The child is no longer some brat from a dysfunctional family but rather a member of the teacher's family. Such a teacher will never be forgotten by his or her students. Because the material being covered in school during those early years is so basic, teachers will not be required to have more advanced technical training. Good teachers will instill the love of knowledge as well as the basic ABCs.

Of course, the next step upward in school is the fourth grade. The era we live in requires knowing computer technology. An inexpensive personal computer *on every desk* would stimulate the overall economy as well as giving each child the main tool for learning. By the end of the fourth grade, every child should know how to travel safely on the "information highway." (Perhaps this subject should be called "Hard Drivers Ed.") Soon there will be no jobs available for those who do not understand basic computer terminology and technology. Once children understand that all information is just a few strokes away on the keyboard, they will be able to concentrate on future careers. Courses like history and geography can effectively be designed to incorporate computer use. Find a place of interest on Google Maps, zoom in to the area under study, and learn something about both history and geography. Breathe some life into these subjects, and the children will soon learn more about their personal surroundings and their place within this world.

From this point on, most (expensive and heavy) school books should be replaced by computer disks that the student can keep at the end of the year. Each student could develop a personal library of disks for future reference work that would require a minimal amount of storage space.

Next, the children enter the years of puberty leading to adolescence. Peer pressure is on the rise. The need to be a part of something becomes evident. Urban children often find their way into gangs. Rural children are more likely to be members of a local 4-H Club or to join a scouting program. Teachers will be tested to their limits, for these are the years that will try their souls.

Gang membership can be useful if they are good gangs. Gangs can be of use in civic programs such as "Street Angels." These activities are normally extracurricular in nature. These positive activities should be designed to help young people make better choices. Why not give such activities a civics class grade in school? Could such a program be more worthwhile than learning about ancient history?

As the children enter the fifth, sixth, seventh, and eighth grades, a more creative way of delivering learning material should be employed. It is a reality that some children are naturally brighter than others. They mature at different times. The brighter students become bored more easily. If held back, many become more aggressive and disruptive. By eliminating the formal grade structure and inaugurating a credit system, it might be possible to harness their energy.

Rather than focusing on a given grade, let us consider a credit system. For example: each successfully completed course equals five credits. Six courses equal the equivalent of one year of schooling. Thirty credits equals one year of school. Twenty-four courses complete the four-year requirement for entrance into high school. The courses are computer-driven (material mainly on disks). This allows each student to select courses of interest, with the main instruction coming from the disks. A teacher qualified in a basic course of instruction (science, humanities, language, etc.) would be available for individual guidance. Such a teacher would spend a few minutes each day with each student making certain all questions were being addressed.

This would require each school system to provide a smorgasbord of subjects for selection. The students, regardless of age (rather than grade), would assemble in one classroom with a highly-qualified teacher. This may somewhat resemble the one-room schoolhouse of yesteryear. The size of the student body would determine the size of the class and the number of teachers required. Being able to learn a subject at your own pace has much merit. It pays extra dividends when considering school days missed because of illness. Currently, a school day missed can leave a gap in the learning experience. Perhaps the disk could be taken home during periods of absences. A disk would also provide refresher training in preparation for examinations. This would develop a degree of uniformity throughout the school system—in other words, every student would be exposed to the same material, which would compensate for those less qualified or emergency substitute teachers.

At present, we rank students by test score, and those can vary from school district to school district, from state to state, yet the material covered in class may be far from uniform. The disk represents a more level playing field—a higher attainable standard.

Why change the current system? Forcing young people to take courses that they hate or feel will never do them any good creates an antilearning experience. Perhaps this is but one factor creating so many school dropouts. An eager-to-learn mind is like a sponge—it absorbs a great deal. Taking desired courses would give the student a sense of controlling his or her own destiny.

Each state school system must have a say in what, if any, courses are required as part of its smorgasbord. Each state may well like to choose a course on the history of its particular state. Agricultural states may wish to have a few courses on basic agriculture, and so forth. Let us not forget courses on civic responsibilities, such as the importance of voting.

Now we must concern ourselves with high school. Each state would develop a more advanced smorgasbord of disks using the same approach as before, only the curriculum becomes more directional. Courses can be targeted to promote future educational opportunities. Others can teach how to cope with life without regard to more advanced academic training. For the more gifted students who desire further education aimed at some profession, there should be preuniversity courses on the menu. High school diplomas for such children would indicate that they graduated with honors and are ready to advance academically. Those less studious would receive a diploma indicating they simply graduated—to adulthood.

No mention has been made thus far concerning extracurricular activities, such as the arts and physical education or sports. Physical activity cannot be replaced by computer disks, and it must be part of the overall educational process. Students must be aware of the need to have healthy bodies in order to enjoy a full life, so time outside the normal classroom should be part of the routine school day. Team sports teach cooperation as well as sportsmanship. Learning how to interact with others is an important aspect of living. Such activities could be considered one of the six courses required each year. The level of activity can be regulated to fit individual needs. Such activities might be well suited for the last class of the day. Perhaps this could be used to address the problems associated with those previously mentioned latchkey children. They would be involved in a healthy supervised activity nearing the time the parents arrive home.

The state smorgasbord of disks might well include basic blue-collar trade disks developed with union input. Such courses would be beneficial for apprentice training in needed professions (a sneaky way to teach geometry to potential carpenters). There should be courses on managing money, writing checks, balancing checkbooks, changing a tire, replacing a lightbulb, or changing a diaper.

Parenthood comes without a manual. Perhaps a course explaining all the work associated with being a parent would result in fewer teenage pregnancies. Let us not forget courses on hygiene and first aid. These courses should be meaningful and aimed at surviving in the real world. Endless worthwhile material is now available on these subjects on the Internet.

Not all children can become suitable college students. In a practical sense, we will always need citizens to dig ditches and take in laundry. Let us not force square pegs into round holes. Allow each student to achieve his or her own niche in life—this too is part of individual freedom. One great feature of our system is that if you make a poor choice early in life, you can normally overcome the negative consequences through determination and hard work.

Up to this point, we have been considering the needs of the average or normal student. We must give thought to those children who do not fall within the "normal" range. Unfortunately, approximately 10 percent of all children have some form of mental, emotional, and/or physical problems that must be addressed. These special children require special attention. The cause and nature of their problems are numerous—they cannot be lumped into any one group or category. Each school district would have to evaluate each such student and provide educational opportunities at an appropriate level. Creating smaller classes, with a teacher trained in dealing with such developmental problems would be an appropriate first step.

No mention has been made of post–high school education. The federal government offers grants and loans to students who request financial assistance in order to further their education. A more educated country is necessary for a more prosperous future. Can you think of any private entity that could do more in this regard? Is the attempt to furnish higher education the work of a sinister and oppressive Big Brother government? One would think an evil government would want to subdue its citizens through ignorance. If you believe our federal government should not be involved in education—then what alternative would you suggest to solve these problems?

My generation is guilty of using the television set as a babysitter. Today's generation is allowing its children to exercise their fingers and thumbs in a quest to win some mindless game. As a result, we have very overweight children, with strong fingers, who cannot live with their own thoughts. They are connected in one way or another with a handheld device sending mundane messages to friends. Perhaps we should blame the parents and not the school system for poor results. If parents are neglecting their children, then perhaps it is time for big government to step in and preserve our nation. Maybe it will *take a village* to save us from ourselves.

Gun Control

The Second Amendment to our Constitution is one of the smallest Amendments contained in our Bill of Rights. It establishes a militia, thus giving the people the right to keep and bear arms. The Amendment is simply stated, leaving no cause for misinterpretation. Unfortunately, it has become the focus of much debate and disagreement. Many people throughout the world think of Americans as a bunch of gun-toting cowboys or gangsters because of our love relationship with firearms. The National Rifle Association lobbies strongly for the right of its members to own guns. It's the doves verses the hawks in this never-ending dispute. Because of the divisive nature of this disagreement, it is a matter worthy of discussion.

We should begin with a reality check. We are a relatively new nation, conceived in war, whose people crossed a wilderness, subduing the sometimes hostile inhabitants. Food was put on the table through hunting. A gun of some fashion was never more than a few feet away from those early pioneers. This is our history, and guns have been with us all the way. The caveman had his club—we have our guns!

The Second Amendment mentions both a militia and the right to bear arms in the same sentence. Self-protection was at the core of this amendment. Our Founding Fathers were not only thinking about hostile natives on the frontier; they had concerns that a foreign government might one day attack our nation (which did happen in 1812!). Self-protection is a noble action. If one person kills another in self-defense, it is not considered murder and is therefore not punishable by law. Gun ownership should not be considered a crime. Individual gun ownership by the masses should give any foreign enemy pause before thinking about invading this land. They would have to understand that it would be a fight for every square inch of ground—from door to door. If any rogue politician should ever desire to establish a dictatorship, he too would have to realize the consequences of his actions.

Guns do not kill without a human finger on the trigger. Unfortunately, that finger is often attached to the body of someone unfit to carry a weapon. A civilized society requires a certain number of rules and regulations in this regard. Generally, a gun kept on private property should be allowed without restriction. The enforceable rules and regulations would apply only to those weapons carried or transported in public.

Sworn police officers and security guards should require special training and certification. Guns being transported from place to place should be disassembled, with the ammunition kept in a different location (e.g., disassembled gun in the car, ammunition in the trunk). Road rage and alcoholism can result in dangerous situations—adding a gun to the equation can only make matters worse.

Perhaps certain weapons such as submachine guns, AK-47s, bazookas, and the like should require some form of registration, since they go way beyond the ordinary requirements for self-defense in a civilized society.

More and more children are taking weapons from their homes and bringing them to school, with serious consequences. Parents of those children should be charged with a felony and severely fined, and the weapon should perhaps be confiscated while there are children in the home. Parents should have a choice between gunlocks or a disassembled weapon. The responsibility should be on the heads of the adults for the misconduct of their children. Perhaps manufacturers of weapons could offer a free video at the time of sale concerning "How to clean your gun without shooting your spouse." The number of persons shot while cleaning a weapon is mind-boggling.

A gun in safe hands isn't such a bad idea. Guns in the hands of drug addicts, alcoholics, irresponsible youth, gangsters, and the mentally disturbed leaves much to be desired. Legislation aimed at curbing weaponry from the socially or mentally unfit is necessary. Any unauthorized person found with a firearm in his or her possession while out in public should be fined, booked, and fingerprinted. Anyone found guilty of possessing a firearm while in the process of committing a crime should be automatically sentenced to life imprisonment. Will such actions completely solve the problem? No, but one hopes that those who can still think rationally will leave their guns at home.

Here is a point for those who reject all forms of gun control to ponder: is the Second Amendment any more or less important with regard to personal freedom than any of the other Amendments? The correct answer should be—all Amendments, as stated in the Bill of Rights, are of equal importance, as they relate to our personal freedoms. (In theory, if the Second Amendment is the most important, why wasn't it made the First Amendment?) As noted in part 1, all social freedoms require a measure of give-and-take in order to ensure that the maximum allowable freedom is afforded to every citizen.

Should reason fail to prevail, then perhaps splitting hairs will become necessary. This could be achieved by allowing ownership and the carrying of guns without restriction, but restrict carrying ammunition while not on private property. Unloaded guns would eliminate unwarranted shootings.

There is an old cliché concerning fighting fire with fire. Let's hope we can eliminate fighting guns with guns. Many gang members currently possess more firepower than the average law enforcement officer has at his or her disposal. We must not return to the days of the Wild West. Let us be reasonable by coming to a mutual understanding as to what is best for our society—what is best for the common good.

This next segment is designed to help citizens understand:

How Government Works

(Surely someone will make fun of this heading!)

Humor is good medicine for the sick and weary. As a life-long government employee, I have learned to laugh at myself and many of my fellow coworkers from time to time. We have made our fair share of mistakes and have been the butt of many a joke. If one takes oneself too seriously, one is lacking a sense of reality. We all (this includes every citizen) have made mistakes, for that is part of being human.

It is hoped that we can come to a higher level of understanding regarding our government. Some forms of government are to be feared—ours should not be. Our form of government is, and will always be, controlled by the vote of its people; many others are not. We often contribute to problem areas by supporting stupidity or failing to exercise our right to vote. There are sins of commission and there are sins of omission. As Edmund Burke (1729–97) said, "For evil to be triumphant, good people need to do nothing."

When we speak ill of our government, we should avoid generalizations. Target the cause of the complaint by being specific. Condemn what is wrong, and praise what is right. If we identify a problem, it can be fixed. By generalizing, we tear ourselves apart, and the problem at hand will never be resolved. Soon "we the People" becomes "them and us." The strings of unity begin to unravel, and freedom suffers. Now let us switch to the nuts and bolts of operating our form of government.

In this land of law and order, we are faced with numerous restrictions—referred to as laws, rules, and regulations. Under the category of laws, we find two major types: constitutional and statutory. The US Supreme Court presides over matters pertaining to constitutional law, while the House and Senate enact all statutory laws. The fifty states follow a similar distinction between their respective constitutional and statutory laws.

Statutory laws are often vague in many areas, thus allowing room for exceptions. (Everyone has heard the old cliché that there is always an exception to any rule.) Statutory laws normally require some form of administration or enforcement. Such laws spell out who has the authority to administer that particular law. Those who are elected, or those who are appointed administrators, set forth the rules and regulations that govern each particular law—such rules and regulations are referred to as "regulatory" laws. These officials are responsible to both Congress and the White House. The top administrators are considered the heads of each agency. They are appointed to their positions by the president, with the consent of the US Senate. They enjoy what is termed political clout. The head of each agency is given a title, such as chairman, director, administrator, or commissioner.

The point should be made that these individuals may not be true federal civil servants, for many are political hacks. This is not meant to be a snide remark but rather a definition of a member of a political party. These appointed individuals come and go with each presidential administration. Oftentimes these appointments can become nothing more than patronage positions wherein the person appointed receives a title and a paycheck for past loyalty and services rendered to the president's political party or objectives. The smart ones are content with the prestige and salary afforded by the appointment—they never rock the boat or accomplish anything worthwhile. The less intelligent ones attempt to make changes over a subject they know little or nothing about. The results can be demoralizing and counterproductive!

The Foreign Service is spared many of these problems because of signed agreements and treaties with other governments. Foreign Service personnel make every effort not to rock the boat in order to maintain stability throughout the world. To such treaties our country's word of honor applies—not political whim. Often a signed treaty will keep an administration from uttering its true beliefs on domestic issues.

This is a good time to introduce the much-belied bureaucrat. A true bureaucrat is someone who follows a law in a rigid manner. A good bureaucrat will not bend the law, take a shortcut, or circumvent the intent of the law. The bureaucrat is often portrayed as someone who lacks common sense. Perhaps there is a need to reevaluate this thinking.

The bureaucrat insists that the i be dotted and the t crossed—doing things right can be a nuisance! (This is often referred to as red tape.) The letter of the law must be obeyed!

Why have laws if they are not to be followed? Should we be governed by *whim*? In all fairness to the bureaucrat, he or she should be commended for doing his or her job properly. Give me a good and honest bureaucrat over someone who fails to watch the store any day. If we must have laws, they should be obeyed, and everyone must be treated equally under the law.

The bureaucrat's job is to protect the law—not make life easy for the sleazy! I wore the title of bureaucrat proudly for several decades believing I was a guardian of the public trust. If a bureaucrat believes that a miscarriage of justice is taking place, he or she must speak out against any injustice as part of his or her fiduciary responsibility. Sometimes bureaucrats' continued employment with the government can be at stake if they speak out against the president or his policies. The choice can be between serving the president of the United States and serving the people of the United States. An honorable bureaucrat will choose the law over political correctness. (Please read the appendix to part 4, which illustrates this point.)

In today's world many citizens take great pleasure in condemning government as being the cause of all our problems. This is because government is big and faceless. It is easy to dislike someone you do not know or are unable to identify. To fix a problem it must be properly identified. Is the complaint aimed at the federal government, or is it perhaps aimed at the state or local government? Which branch of government is causing the person's ire? Is the problem caused by a bureaucrat or an elected official? Is it because of a particular law, or is the citizen just venting because of frustration? In the military they have an expression—*SNAFU*—which is understood by all service personnel, and it says it all.

If we have a genuine complaint, we should be specific as to what part of government is at fault. The shotgun approach—damning all of government—weakens the argument and serves no useful purpose. Identify the exact source of frustration. Then, and only then, can the problem be addressed and possibly resolved. Should we blame all grocery stores for something that happened in one such store?

Some citizens fear that a sinister Big Brother government will somehow develop and take away our liberties. Others dislike the restrictions placed upon us by so many laws, rules, and regulations. Everyone hates taxation, and it is government that is the cause of taxation. Just say the word *government* or *taxes*—eyes will roll, heads will shake, and the all-knowing nodding of the head tells everyone present that they fully understand that the problem is caused by the damn government. It becomes the civilian counterpart of the military's SNAFU situation.

Chances are that most of the frustration stems from problems initiated at the state or local levels of government. Local governments have a daily and more direct impact on the affairs of the average citizen. Permits, licenses, local rules, and regulations affect us more frequently than anything that might transpire in far-off Washington, DC.

There are more than sixty small, independent agencies within our federal government under the administrative control of the Chief Executive. These are in addition to the huge departments headed by members of the cabinet. Pinpointing the source of a problem can be difficult. Difficult if we are attempting to fix a problem!

Here is a point to ponder. For every complaint leveled against the government, there are ten times more that could be applied to the private sector. The problem lies in the fact that we have humans working in government as well as in the private sector. A government employee may say or do something that annoys us. Has this ever happened in a retail store? With a store employee, we look down upon that store or the individual employee. If it is a government employee, we tend to damn the entire government.

Here is another point to ponder. It would be extremely difficult for any one government employee or official to do serious damage to our society. One civil servant simply does not possess that much power. If any government employee is found to be a wrongdoer, he or she will be punished and removed from office post haste. If a government employee makes a mistake, the government usually provides compensation for any loss caused by the actions of one of its employees.

Can this be said of wrongdoing in the private sector? (Ken Lay of the former Enron Corporation; Robert Keating of the Lincoln Savings and

Loan Association; Michael Milken, the junk bond whiz; and Bernard Madoff, the Ponzi king, are but a handful of individuals who have hurt hundreds, perhaps thousands, of investors.) There is little hope that those investors will receive compensation for their losses. Wrongdoing individuals in the private sector can cause more problems than any one civil servant could ever dream of doing.

It is safer to place our faith in government than to trust those motivated by greed. On the lighter side, the government has long proven to be a nonprofit organization; therefore there is far less greed in government as compared to the private sector. Most government employees are motivated by public service and not by riches or bottom-line profits. If they desired riches, the last place they would seek employment would be with the government.

Here are examples of that statement. A young high school graduate can obtain a far better salary working at a bank than being employed by the government doing the same type of work. This applies to all levels of employment. Compare the salary (with or without perks) of a treasurer of any single major corporation against the salary of the Treasurer of the entire United States of America. Compare the salary of the FBI Director against the salary of a chief security officer for any major private corporation. High pay is simply not a motivator for a federal employee. On the other hand, perceived perks are important motivators for higher echelon employees. Such perks can lead to waste. This is also true in the private sector.

Many worry over waste within government. Civil servants who do not honor their position of trust should be removed from office immediately. There is a real need to keep an eye on procurement agencies and sections of the military establishment responsible for procurement. So-called sweetheart deals are often made during procurement activities.

There is also much waste within the judicial branch of government because the legislative branch cannot interfere with the budget demands of the judicial branch. The judicial branch has little or no worry over budgetary restrictions. Judges enjoy a virtual carte blanche expense account when it comes to acquiring office space and other such needs.

As good Americans we tend to go all-out in support of our military personnel by giving them what they need and want. This approach opens the door for waste and abuse to enter the system. With every squeeze of the trigger, a round is spent—each spent round carries a price tag. A semiautomatic weapon can evaporate a twenty-dollar bill in seconds. War is costly, and this is but one more reason why it should be avoided.

We have all heard of expensive hammers and toilet seats costing unreasonable amounts. Such items do not actually cost that much, so the amount shown is designed to hide missing funds. It is impossible to account for every item charged to the military, and we must therefore give special attention to President Eisenhower's warning to be wary of the military-industrial complex.

Here are a few facts to consider: there are nearly forty four-star generals and admirals currently on active duty. Eighty percent of these extremely high-ranking officers will find employment with defense contractors upon retirement. Did someone use the word *cozy*?

Flag officers in all branches of the armed forces are treated as potentates, each with their own private fiefdom. Perks are of utmost importance to any flag officer. Each has a personal staff consisting not only of gold-braided military aides, but also those who are little more than servants. We dare not call such enlisted personnel butlers so they are referred to as orderlies. They say rank has its privileges! Privileges cost money, and this begs the question: Do we absolutely require so many high-ranking (four-star) officers within the military establishment?

The military mind-set thrives on pomp and circumstance. There are more displays of this form of behavior within the military than in any other segment of our society. In many parts of the world, May Day is celebrated with much military fanfare. Flags wave, bands beat a military cadence, while thousands of troops and various pieces of military hardware pass in review. These are grand displays of pride and nationalism. Wouldn't it be wonderful to see teams of doctors and nurses pushing hospital beds down the street? They could be followed by interns beating on bedpans or perhaps teachers pushing blackboards. Surely such professionals deserve our support and applause as well. (This may appear to be a silly thought—but it is the essence of thought that deserves a measure of consideration.) Let us now leave our thoughts about the military and return to the civilian side of government.

Here is what happens when a new civilian government agency is created: Congress passes a law that includes the creation of a new agency in order to administer this new law. Up to this point there are no living employees who know anything about this new law—simply because it is new. People apply for positions within this new agency through the Office of Personnel Management. They are screened, examined, tested, and subjected to background checks. From this pool of candidates, the most qualified are selected for employment. Education and past experiences are important considerations for employment. Once hired, this group of inexperienced employees begins to formulate organizational charts. They create a series of manuals that include position descriptions. They are flying by the seat of their pants—learning and making things up as they go along. The extremely bright employees are placed on the fast track in terms of promotions. Are mistakes made during this process? Of course! When a law is that new, there is no one around who fully understands all the aspects associated with that law. Mistakes are bound to happen!

The most recently created government agency was the Department of Homeland Security. Shortly after 9/11, thousands of previously employed privately contracted airport screeners became federal employees overnight. Many of these ill-trained and misguided employees made a considerable number of blunders during those early days as they attempted to follow new official guidelines. Elderly persons were subjected to strip searches and other ridiculous procedures. As time goes on, fewer and fewer mistakes will be made. Let us call this "employment evolution" and refrain from condemning the entire government. This sort of thing happens in privately owned stores and shops across America all the time. Much learning in life occurs through trial and error. Lack of experience is a major cause of many a blunder in both government and the private sector.

Let us switch our focus to those well-established agencies that have been around for quite some time. Higher-ranking managers within every unit of an agency are given an annual operating budget. These managers normally set some money aside for unexpected events. Some money is set aside for training. Some set money aside in order to conduct audits and inspections of the various units under their supervision. The vast majority of the budget is applied toward carrying out the main mission of the agency—for, after all, that is why the agency was created.

Now enters a new political administration bent on reducing government spending. A directive is issued ordering all agencies to reduce their budgets by 10 percent. Every budget official reviews his or her assigned budget in order to determine where the cuts can best be made. They cannot make cuts to the main purpose of their existence, so they attack areas where they hope they can get along without for a period of time. Emergency contingencies are among the first to go. Training might be next. Inspections and auditing will soon follow. With each cut, fingers will be crossed, with the hope that nothing will go wrong as a result of these cutbacks.

Without internal inspections it is only a matter of time before bridges collapse, contaminated produce enters the food chain, and mad cow disease is discovered, and of course the government will be blamed when things go wrong. There are two old sayings: "You get what you pay for" and "There is no such thing as a free lunch." Cut back on government spending, and negative things will begin to happen—it is only a matter of time. If inspections and audits were unnecessary, they would not be done in the first place.

Here is another example of what happens when government is not allowed to perform its assigned duties properly: a few years ago the Security Exchange Commission (SEC) was found to be negligent in its oversight duties. Guess what happened? The same cut-back mentality was in play, oversights occurred, and the government was damned once again. No one should run a business or oversee a law half-heartedly. We must either fund programs properly or suffer the consequences. Cutting back on rules and regulations is much like leaving a henhouse unprotected. Predators will enter disguised as free-enterprise entrepreneurs and devour the flock one by one.

Here are some more points to ponder. We take so many things for granted. There are little things that control our daily conduct. Take, for instance, the street intersection nearest your home that has a functioning traffic control light. When the light is red, we are forced to stop (taking away from our freedom). When the light turns green, we are free to go forward. Yellow tells us to be cautious! Who controls that light? Who owns that light? Yes, you guessed right—it is owned and operated by the local government. But wait—the government is "we the people"; therefore, we own the traffic light. We turned the control of that light over to a government agency in order to promote safety. We did so in the name of the common good! Please imagine a large city with no traffic lights during rush hour. Surely the reader will understand the point being made—we and government are one and the same.

At that same intersection, we find street signs. Some tell us the direction of the street and how far it is from the center of the town. Please imagine a large city without street signs. Again, you get the picture! In small farm communities such signs might not exist. Those citizens give and get directions by identifying simple landmarks.

That is an example of why people living outside of metropolitan areas have less need for government. This example also makes it easy to understand why we are being called a nation divided. It is not a simple case of Republicans versus Democrats, or north versus south, or liberals versus conservatives. We are divided because we do not understand each other's basic needs. Rural citizens don't need or want intrusive government. Urban citizens cannot coexist without it. Someday small towns will become big towns and attitudes will change in those areas. Many city dwellers wish they had less need for government involvement in their lives. This is where realism comes into play. Over time, with an ever-growing population, government will become a more important part of living. We can either fight reality or roll with the punches!

Many believe that governmental social programs represent socialism. While such programs might be considered somewhat socialistic in nature, they are not part of our economic system, which is capitalism. Social programs will not turn us into socialists. Perhaps such negative believers should try to understand the true meaning and definition of socialism.

In true socialism, the government owns and operates businesses, and the people benefit from the output of those businesses. Socialism can be both a form of government and an economic system. The United States is a democratic republic with capitalism as its economic engine. All governments own public property in one form or another. Those traffic lights and signs mentioned earlier are owned and operated by the government, and the people share in the beneficial results. The same is true of all public roads within the United States. These are not businesses and are therefore not part of an economic system. Government ownership of public property or involvement in humanitarian entitlement programs does not make us socialists. With few exceptions, the majority of all governments throughout the world attempt to feed their starving people. These are not socialistic countries—these are humanistic services provided by government for the benefit of the citizens of that country.

We must come to the understanding that government involvement in our lives will not turn our democratic republic into some other form of government. By following the Constitution, with its many amendments, we will preserve our freedoms to the maximum degree possible. This takes us back to points made in part 1 regarding our understanding of freedom.

In reviewing the contents of part 2, we have covered two major areas. The first was an attempt to bring understanding to economic issues. It is economic issues that are exacerbating the differences between political parties. The purpose of this book is to have both sides step back and look at the problem in a different light, thus finding more common ground through better understanding. Trying to minimize the usefulness of government in a large, complex, industrial society such as ours is not going to bring about prosperity. In fact it will result in just the opposite outcome.

The second area of part 2 relates to a host of issues that currently add to our discord. For the most part these are social issues, and, while they are a source of contention, they will not cause our system of government to fall apart. Being able to disagree is part of belonging to a democracy. In this regard we should attempt to approach all areas of disagreement with civility. Open and honest discussion promotes understanding and helps to ensure consensus on vital issues.

It is now time to peer into the future. Are you ready?

PART 3
Hopes and Aspirations

Toward the Future

As we head into the uncertainties of tomorrow, we must remind ourselves that several current duties and responsibilities need to be carried over into the future. Such topics are not original—just absolutely necessary in order to retain and maintain our form of government.

We must be realistic and accept change as inevitable. Demographics will continue to change. Technology will change. Research and other developments will occur. Knowledge will increase. Many of our attitudes about a variety of issues will change. We must be as flexible as possible by avoiding unnecessary rigidity. We must exercise a degree of caution in that all changes need not be inherently good. Let us begin this segment by emphasizing the importance of:

The All-Important Vote

In a free land, there can be nothing more sacred than the vote. It expresses the will of the people. It is the essence of a democracy and a republic. To manipulate the outcome of elections in a democracy is tantamount to treason. If any voting process leaves doubt as to the outcome, it must be addressed, reviewed, and corrected. To do less invites skepticism and distrust and can lead to anarchy.

The United States of America is looked upon as the leader of honest elections, yet there have been instances indicating our system is less than perfect. The presidential elections of 1960 and 2000 are examples of questionable outcomes. Such situations should never exist. What causes such doubt? We must look for a cause and correct it. One cause is very obvious—it is a lack of uniformity. Each of our fifty states is allowed to create its own ballot system; hence, we have fifty ways of producing a ballot. Making matters worse, within each state there are numerous ways to vote, thereby creating more possible negative outcomes.

Perhaps individual states should have the right to process their own elections as they see fit. It is the vote for all federal officeholders that should require absolute uniformity. There must be one, and only one, set of rules for handling national elections. If good results are expected for state elections, then each individual state must comply with the principles of uniformity. In truth, there should be but one criterion for all federal, state, and local elections—if there is to be confidence in the election process.

"Stuffing the ballot box" means filling a ballot box with illegal votes. (In Chicago, my hometown, the saying was "Vote early and often.") A much more honorable meaning would be to stuff the ballot box with legal votes. The more citizens who vote will result in a more meaningful election. If one doesn't vote, one should give up the right to complain or criticize. Apathy in this regard should be considered un-American. Many have died in order to give us the right to vote. The least we can do is to cast a ballot to honor their sacrifices.

Once again I would like to make a personal observation. As a federal employee, I have lived and voted in six different states. I have voted in fire stations, retirement club houses, garages, and schools. Ballot procedures differed greatly from place to place. We used ballpoint pens in one state, number 2 pencils in another, and indelible markers in yet another. There have been paper ballots, punch cards (with and without hanging chads), machines with mechanical levers, and electronic machines. The cost of operating such polling places is significant. Those who oversee the polling places are paid. There is nothing that resembles uniformity between the various states.

The current method used in the state of Oregon appears worthy of national consideration. It is more cost effective than most other systems. The results are verifiable because of the paper trail left behind after each election. The final tabulation may take longer to certify than electronic ballots, but it is worth the wait. The final certification falls well within the time limits set forth in the Constitution. We must remember that the presidential inauguration takes place more than two months after the election—plenty of time for several recounts. Time is not of the essence! Let the various news networks fill their time slots with more newsworthy items while waiting for the results of the election.

A great travesty occurred during the presidential election of 2000 in the state of Florida, making a sham of that state's election procedures. Our country became the butt of many jokes throughout the world. Just when you think politics has hit an all-time low, something like that happens. Those shenanigans brought to our attention another unique feature in our election system—the Electoral College provision as outlined in the Constitution (Article II, Section 1).

The Electoral College

What is the Electoral College? Why is it in our Constitution?

Prior to the election of George Washington, the members of the Continental Congress met and voted on a leader. They picked one of their own members to be their leader—giving that person the title of president. (The majority party within the British parliamentary system selects the officers of the government while they are in power. The people of Great Britain do not directly elect their prime minister.) George Washington was the first president to be elected by the vote of the *people* and not by the members of Congress.

During the process of formalizing the Constitution a disagreement arose among the members. Some wanted the Congress to elect the president, while others wanted the people to elect the president. The Electoral College idea came into existence as a compromise. The vote of the people was to be incorporated into the concept of the Electoral College. The fear was based on the assumption that one or two largely populated states could elect the president, leaving the other smaller states out in the cold. One has to keep in mind that the year was 1787, and many of the states were quite small (Rhode Island, Delaware, and Connecticut). The expressed concern was justifiable for that time period. Need it apply today?

Historical footnote: Since the beginning of our country and prior to the election of 2000 there have been only three presidential candidates who won the presidency without winning the majority (51 percent) of the popular vote of the people. They were John Quincy Adams (1824); Rutherford B. Hayes (1876); and finally Benjamin Harrison (1888). Can the reader see how fragmentation weakens the office of the president?

In the year 2000, the Democratic presidential candidate, Al Gore, received a larger national popular vote than did the Republican candidate, George W. Bush. Mr. Bush became president because of the Electoral College and not by the majority vote of the people. Many citizens objected to this outcome, arguing that the total vote of the people should have outweighed the Electoral College. Because of our changing demographics, those early concerns of our Founding Fathers are much less likely to apply in this day and age. The Constitution would have to be amended in order to remove that section pertaining to the Electoral College. Many believe that every individual vote should count, and they would therefore support such an amendment.

Review of Priorities

As I stated in the opening segment of this book, we all desire as much personal freedom as possible. For all of us to enjoy an equal level of freedom, we must be willing to compromise—with emphasis on the word *willing*. This level of freedom comes only through the obedience to law. In the future, as in the past, we must obey all laws, rules, and regulations enacted by our elected officials. Laws can be changed; but until then, they must be obeyed.

We understand the all-important aspect of unity—for without unity we will fail as a nation. Without unity we would no longer be a superpower. We must lift one another up and not tear each other apart if we are to succeed as "one nation under God." It is therefore imperative that we make every attempt to get along with our fellow countrymen. We can disagree and be civil at the same time. Grandmother used to say, "If you can't be big, don't belittle!"

Those with short fuses show a lack of personal restraint (self-control). Ignorance ignites a short fuse; therefore, we must wise up, learn to count to ten, take a deep breath, and try to understand the other person's point of view.

As our general population grows, so must our government. We desire to keep the finer aspects of capitalism as our economic engine—while understanding the forces of greed that can lead to domination within our society. We want to continue working within a free enterprise system. Our government should be allowed to assist the nation in economic matters whenever absolutely necessary. Government should never own or operate businesses, for that would be socialism if it became common practice. Uncontrolled capitalism would eventually cause the people to be manipulated by giant corporations and extremely rich individuals. We must rein in greed—as un-capitalistic as that may sound to some.

In the future we must rein in fear, especially as it applies to fiscal issues. Many of us worry more than necessary over monetary matters. Such thoughts erode consumer confidence and tend to make matters worse. Remember, politicians love to create fear in order to win votes. Some politicians and candidates for office become fixated on the deficit, yet they are unable to do anything constructive about it. We, the people, have as much, if not more, control over the deficit than do politicians. We can do so by understanding the reasoning outlined in my concept of the domestic spending cycle.

We desire to maintain our democratic republic form of government for as long as humanly possible. We understand that the key to our economic success as a nation hinges on employment. We must create employment opportunities as fast as our population grows. We want a particular type of a have and have-not society—in that we want to have work and not have unemployment.

Needed Modifications

If we wish to improve government, we should consider the following: (1) elimination of the electoral college concept from the Constitution, thereby making every vote count; (2) gerrymandering congressional districts should be eliminated at the state level and the voting procedures for elective federal offices should be standardized; (3) the theory of individual collectivism should be revisited by the Supreme Court with the intent to curtail the negative aspects of lobbying. Corporations and unions should not be considered equal to the individual; (4) the seating arrangements in both houses of Congress should be modified—away from political party lines and more toward the representation of states and individuals; (5) and the executive branch should not have the power to deregulate any law passed by the legislative branch. Keeping politics out of regulations will be in the best interests of the common good. Political tampering with regulations will only weaken a law. Weak laws will never enhance the common good.

The above recommendations will not change our form of government or our economic system. These changes simply fine-tune our democracy, making us a little more democratic and responsive to the needs of the people.

In part 2 we considered the many problems and disagreements we face at this point in time. We need to revisit those problems and attempt to find solutions for them as we sail into the sunrise of a new day.

Troublemakers

Prejudice, by definition, means to "prejudge." Our prejudices are often the result of past experiences or the teachings of others. They can be stimulated by a "gut feeling" or be part of a moral belief system. In order to overcome prejudice, one must keep an open mind. That is a mind capable of entertaining new thoughts based on facts and rational reasoning. Does the reader possess an open, a narrow, or a completely closed mind?

We need only to gaze into a mirror to see a reflection of imperfection. It is we the people, as our government, who are the cause of many problems. Citizens should be willing to accept a fair share of blame for government mistakes.

According to Sigmund Freud (1856–1939), the founder of modern psychoanalysis, mankind is comprised of three entities: the id; the ego; and the superego. There are enumerable variables within all three entities. These elements add to the complexity of understanding our fellow human beings.

Many people function at a near animal level—we encounter such individuals almost daily. Some cannot help themselves; others prefer to feed their earthly desires rather than think about the consequences of their actions.

Those who use their brains can make both right and wrong choices. We often learn life's lessons the hard way. As humans, we are allowed to be wrong from time to time. The trick is making good choices that will last a lifetime and beyond. In terms of government, how can we be assured that we are making good choices? We can begin by heeding that still, small voice from within—often referred to as our conscience. When we think of others before self, we lessen our chances of succumbing to the seven deadly sins—pride, envy, anger, sloth, avarice, gluttony, and lust.

Avarice, more commonly known as greed, plays a major part in uncontrolled capitalistic thinking. If capitalism is not harnessed, it will consume us. The foremost question to be asked of ourselves is this: Can we change our behavior? Changing human nature is extremely difficult. It cannot be accomplished by any one person, yet that is where it must begin. If we want to be the very best we can be, we must become united in purpose. We must become less self-centered and focus our attention on the common good.

The material presented in this book supports government involvement in economic matters *whenever necessary.* According to many economists, the recent stimulus packages, designed to help businesses during a financial crisis, are an acceptable function of government. But in contrast to the precepts of the Keynesian theory, taxation need not be decreased if it results in overall social improvements. We must remember—taxation could control the size of the deficit if used to pay down the debt.

While we can tolerate a national debt, we must come to realize that personal debt is unhealthy for us as individuals. Our personal balance sheets must be kept in order. A personal credit rating is not viewed in the same way as a government credit rating. Credit card companies are charging outlandish interest rates that no individual should be forced to pay. No citizen should become a slave to credit. We can free ourselves through savings. Credit card interest rates should be based solely on individual credit ratings. If the cardholder is a credit risk, he or she should be charged more or not given credit. Extending more credit to someone who is a known credit risk is much like offering an alcoholic another drink. Credit card companies are charging everyone higher rates in order to recover money lost by borrowing to high-risk individuals. Those companies are risking absolutely nothing as they use credit to enslave others.

How to Improve

If we desire a robust economy, we need to have people working and earning money. We realize that technological advancements make work easier and often decrease the need for physical labor in many sectors. We realize that our population will continue to grow, and therefore there will be fewer jobs per capita available in the future. This can be stated in capitalistic terms involving supply and demand—too few jobs, too many job seekers. Logic tells us that this will adversely affect our society in the long haul. Employment must be manufactured in order to resolve such problems. Who can best create this need for employment? The private sector plays a very important role in this regard once people have money to spend.

To prime the pump, however, the government will have to lead the way. The government, because it is not driven by the bottom-line principles of capitalism, can create employment opportunities by starting projects that might not be financially profitable at the time yet will serve the future needs of the nation. (Refer to earlier comments on future needs for desalinizing plants and improved electrical grids.) The private sector, working under the principles of capitalism by not witnessing a profit, would not become involved in such projects until it was too late. Many of our citizens are reactive, not proactive, in regard to solving problems. Some will wait for their automobile to stop running before having it serviced.

The following subject might draw some favorable reactions! Who set the official work week at forty hours? The Bible indicates that God worked six days and rested on the seventh. So how did we arrive at this forty-hour concept? Is this another man-made idea conceived through compromise? Is the concept of a forty-hour work week etched in stone somewhere—never to be reconsidered? Maybe it is time we looked at our watches once again and reset the time clocks in our shops, offices, and factories.

As our population grows, the need for more job opportunities will eventually outnumber the actual number of jobs available. It would be better to have more people paying into Social Security and Medicare than having them not contribute because of the lack of employment opportunities. So let us be creative and create employment opportunities! Share the wealth by sharing the available work. Americans united and working for the common good could achieve the desired results.

There is no need to have 80 percent of the available work force working and 20 percent unemployed. Make life easier for some and more fulfilling for others by sharing the load. Many will argue that this will cause more inflation. But if greed can be kept under control, so can inflation.

Both the private sector and the government can begin by improving working hours for the betterment of all people. Companies and corporations that currently work around the clock (24/7) are best suited for this suggestion. They could begin by shortening their standard work week from forty hours to thirty-five and then hiring a few more employees to maintain production levels.

Reducing hours would normally result in a loss of wages for those affected by such cutbacks. This could be controlled in different ways. Freeze the wages of current employees for a period of time in order to compensate for hiring additional employees. In some situations, lower wages would result in lower tax withholdings. This would reduce the loss of actual take-home pay. The unions would enjoy an increase in membership and could perhaps lower their dues for a like period of time. Union leaders would need to cooperate in this endeavor by agreeing to refrain from making demands for benefits and wage increases in the short term.

Current workers would have to come to the realization that large numbers of unemployed fellow citizens would cause their personal taxes to increase. (They must remember, once again, that unemployment stifles production, which in turn weakens their own earning potential.) Employees as well as employers must start thinking ahead—they must look at a long-lasting big picture.

A current employer pays his old employees less while creating employment for new employees. This will result in more customers for the future and ensure long-term profits for these major companies. The government receives less tax from the older employees while receiving taxes from the newly employed. The retirement trust funds and Medicare fund are then better funded for the future. Why not slowly, very slowly, begin the process now? If we are going to maintain a strong, middle-class democracy, we will eventually have to come to this level of understanding.

If government, business, and labor worked together in unity, there is nothing they could not accomplish, but each must consider the needs of the other parties. (You may not know your neighbor's name, but you are in the same lifeboat.) This suggestion would ultimately prove to be of benefit to all concerned. This suggestion would be for the *common good.*

There are many issues that keep us from having a more perfect union. More than likely, the most common and serious issue revolves around a lack of education. Ignorance cannot be ignored! It must be contained if we are to be considered an enlightened people. A great nation can ill afford to have large pockets of ignorance existing anywhere within its borders. Ignorance based on superstitions and naïveté must give way to reality. Religious beliefs often restrict secular knowledge. An open mind can enhance the search for knowledge while still holding fast to personal convictions.

All environmental issues must be considered if we are to think about the future. Clean water, pure air, and productive soil should be our legacy to our children and grandchildren. If we destroy our environment, we will, in fact, be destroying future generations. We must become extremely proactive in this regard.

Mature people realize there are limitations to all things. There is little room for wild-eyed extremism in any of human beings' endeavors. Working together in harmony will produce better, more long-lasting results.

For those who oppose any form of gun control, please give this subject more thought. There is good reason for gun ownership, and there is good reason for some level of control. Let us be rational and come to some consensus on this important issue—for our common good.

We must continue to maintain peace through power and not domination. President Teddy Roosevelt said it best: "Speak softly but carry a big stick." A preemptive strike without warning as suggested by President George W. Bush should never be contemplated by our government. It would be a repetition of what happened to our country on December 7, 1941.

We must work closely and in cooperation with our allies before attacking either another sovereign nation or a rogue leader. In the future, if there should ever be another Hitler, that person should be removed from society before unjustifiable suffering is inflicted upon the world. The World Court must find such persons guilty of crimes against humanity and issue a death warrant. That warrant could then be carried out with immunity. Nations must jointly work toward a more united world where we might someday find peace on earth and good will toward men.

Will our national population continue to grow? Of course—that is a realistic assumption. Will we then require more government employees, such as firemen, policemen, school teachers, etc.? Of course—that too is a realistic assumption. With more people, will there be a realistic need for more rules, regulations, and restrictions? Of course—this is likewise a reasonable assumption. Based upon these realistic assumptions, should we be expected to downsize our government? Downsize, no—modernize, yes! With the passage of time, and an ever-changing world, many government agencies may need to be eliminated or combined with other agencies. We need a stable, not a static or stagnant, government.

If we look far into the future, we can reasonably see the need for increased food production; more clean water; and more energy production. Our available farmland will struggle to maintain present-day levels of production as the human population continues to grow. Grazing animals require more land for feed. It might become necessary to eat more pork and fowl (rather than beef) in order to convert grazing land into farmland. More freshwater fisheries may be needed in the future to ensure an abundant supply of edible items and create a major source of protein. More saltwater fishing for species we now avoid may become necessary. Converting lowlands and marshes into rice fields could supplement wheat as a basic staple for life. Finding a way to make coal a clean source of energy might be necessary for generating electricity, thus reducing our dependence on more limited resources.

After all is said and done, we must remain ever vigilant for alternatives, as change is always in the air. We must consider alternatives to every action taken. Let us now step back and take a look at the big picture while considering possible alternatives.

Does the reader fully understand the meaning of freedom and democracy? If you cannot agree with what has been written in this book concerning the benefits of democracy, what is your alternative suggestion?

Do you place individualism ahead of unity? Is one more important than the other? Will one create more freedom than the other? Which serves the principles of democracy best? If you choose individualism, be prepared to move away from the herd of humanity. If you choose unity, you will become part of something greater than yourself. This is perhaps the hardest choice any citizen can make. It pits self-interest against the common good. Are you willing to go it alone? Are you willing to live among 313,338,000 mavericks of one form or other? Or is it possible to live in unity with others and still enjoy an acceptable amount of individualism as outlined in part 1? In that case, unity becomes more essential than individualism. Such a positive decision places you in lockstep with the Founding Fathers. The reader might recall that our Founding Fathers often referred to freedom, liberty, and unity, but do you recall them overtly dwelling upon the virtues of individualism in those early official documents?

As for a form of government: Do you enjoy living in a democratic republic? Or would you prefer to live under a monarch, a dictator, or in a theocracy?

As for an economic system, would you prefer uncontrolled capitalism (you know: dog-eat-dog-style economics), or would you prefer a system less heartless? This should be a simple choice for a true individualist who does not care about others.

There is one more philosophical issue to consider. What is the real meaning of the term "we the people"? Every reader knows what the words are meant to imply, but how does the reader incorporate them into everyday thinking?

We must come to the understanding that government is made up of ordinary human beings, as is the case in the private sector. Some government employees are brighter than others, just as in the private sector. Some will make mistakes, just as in the private sector. Government employees are nothing more than our fellow citizens and countrymen and women. They control parts of our lives just as they are controlled by us. The hardest of all ideas for the majority of our citizens to understand is that our government is, in fact, "we the people"—a bunch of individuals banded together in the quest for freedom.

The big picture is now complete—the dots have been connected. There is still hope for the future—provided we heed this call for unity. This is a growing nation, both in numbers and technical achievements. There will be more interdependence of our people as we seek to promote the common good. We will require a more enlightened population in order to meet the challenges of tomorrow.

What does the reader see? Is the picture still hazy? Does the reader have any other ideas regarding solving the problems outlined in part 2? If so, please share your thoughts and tell us what we might do! Let your voice be heard! For we are all in this together! Finding fault is not the same as constructive criticism. Let's stop complaining and fault-finding, for there is much blame to go around should we wander down that road.

I am reminded of an old cliché: If all else fails, stupid, read the instructions:

"Love thy neighbor as thyself."

This directive (or instruction), the second of two great Christian commandments, was given more than two thousand years ago. (Cynics and hate-mongers detest this admonition.) This directive is not simply a call for love—it is a call for unity. It is a call for unity based on love—not law. It is like unto marriage, wherein individuals become one in spirit. In the long run, we would all benefit from a healthy and prosperous society by heeding such a principle.

May our government continue to grow! May we be our "big brother's keeper" in order to keep him from becoming too big for his britches. Working as a family, in unity with mutual consideration and respect, will enable us to overcome all obstacles. As in all normal families, we can squabble and disagree, but we must do so with civility—exercising both patience and tolerance.

As we sail farther into the future, may we better understand the beauty of life, the strength associated with unity, and continue to experience the joy of maximum allowable freedom. There is no better place to live on this planet than in the *United* States of America. Long may her banner wave!

The following quotation sums up the thoughts expressed in this book:

The American Creed

"I believe in the United States of America as a government of the people, by the people, for the people; whose just powers are derived from the consent of the governed; a democracy in a republic; a sovereign Nation of many sovereign States, a perfect union, one and inseparable; established upon those principles of freedom, equality, justice, and humanity for which American patriots sacrificed their lives and fortune.

"I, therefore, believe it is my duty to my country to love it, to support its Constitution, to obey its laws, to respect its flag, and to defend it against all enemies."

William Tyler Page (1868–1942)
Clerk of the United States House of Representatives

The End?

Postscript: This book does not represent the end but rather the beginning of all tomorrows. This book was written with the future in mind. It outlines the role of the federal government in the twenty-first century. The size of government will increase in direct proportion to our population growth. Our government will be needed in many areas of life if we wish to be considered proactive. *We must make government work for us as we work for our government.* Only through unity can we make great achievements possible.

The maximum amount of freedom is the quest of all humankind—that is our goal and destination. Adherence to law and order is the driving force that will get us there. Unity is the pathway.

As a united people, we will continue to grow and prosper, while the lone rangers among us will ride off into the sunset of obscurity. We must bridle individualism in order to rein in greed and selfishness while harnessing up team spirit and unity.

After reading this book, you are under no obligation to agree with the material stated herein. You still possess the personal freedom of having an opinion. You can accept or reject any or all thoughts herein expressed. If I had my druthers, I would live on a small, sparsely populated island with only friends and relatives of my choosing. I would be free of all responsibilities of any major importance. Alas, I realize my druthers are but dreams associated with wishful thinking—devoid of reality.

Have the opinions expressed in this book gone beyond reality? (A true cynic will say I live in a dream world—as if a character in a fairy tale. Perhaps I am, but isn't that what hope and aspirations are all about?) Negativity (which accomplishes nothing) notwithstanding: Do the expressed thoughts in this book contain a degree of logic and common sense? If I have overlooked something of importance, please do what they say in Missouri: "Show me!" I welcome all thoughts and new ideas—how else can we learn from one another? No individual has all the answers and no individual can solve all of our problems.

I would like to beseech all readers: If you concur with a particular view expressed in this book, please feel free to share it with your three designated representatives in Congress. Ask them to consider giving support to such views. Who knows, they just might read that material and take appropriate and positive action. There may still be some members in Congress who are motivated by the thought of doing something for the *common good*, rather than being guided by political alliances and self-interest.

Now this ancient mariner and proud bureaucrat must bid everyone a bon voyage as he sets sail toward the next promised land.

PART 4
Appendix

Author's testimony before the US House of Representatives, Select Committee on Aging, held in Missoula, Montana, on April 17, 1982:

"My name is William W. Robé. I am the regional director of the US Railroad Retirement Board's Fifth Region, which encompasses the Rocky Mountain and Pacific Coastal States. I am here at the written invitation of Congressman Claude Pepper, Chairman of the Select Committee on Aging.

"The board serves nearly one million aged annuitants and beneficiaries throughout the United States, as well as one half million active railroad employees who are all strung out in the process of aging. Approximately 470 board employees are in the field service responding to the needs of that railroad community. Since 1977 my regional workforce has been reduced by 23 percent, leaving only seventy-six employees to cover one-third of the nation's landmass. Because of the vast distances between towns and cities out here in the West, sufficient travel allowance funding is vital to the level of service we are able to provide the widely-scattered railroad communities.

"Recently, the administration submitted budget proposals to Congress for the forthcoming fiscal year. Everyone by now must know that the administration called for the abolishment of the board and termed our activities an 'inappropriate federal function.' I must object to that statement and ask the following: Is it really an inappropriate federal function? Is it any more or less than the government's involvement in Social Security? The board exists because of a federal law passed by Congress and held constitutional by the US Supreme Court. I believe it would be a totally inappropriate federal response to ignore such a basic fact.

"Many of us in this room feel certain that the administration's proposals will not become a reality, for in order to do so, Congress would have to pass a law changing both the Railroad Retirement Act and the Railroad Unemployment and Sickness Insurance Act. In other words, Congress need only do nothing for the proposals to mean nothing. How I wish the problem would end right there! Unfortunately, the Office of Management and Budget (OMB) currently has authority to limit every federal agency's budget and demand that they reduce their employment ceilings.

"Money and personnel cuts of the magnitude proposed by OMB for this agency during the next fiscal year would reduce my regional workforce by an additional 30 percent and just about bring to a halt our ability to properly serve much of our railroad community. At that point I would have to give serious thought to closing nearly one-half of my district offices. Spokane (which services this portion of Montana) would more than likely be one of those closed, as would Portland and Klamath Falls in Oregon; Boise and Pocatello in Idaho; leaving only Seattle and Billings to cover the entire Northwest. What kind of service are we expected to provide to our elderly, disabled, widowed, sick, and unemployed (of which there are so many nowadays) under such conditions?

"We have thousands on our rolls who were born before the turn of the century. Many are feeble, some no longer competent, some unable to read and write, some without a telephone, some unable to drive or get about easily. Do we ignore their needs? Is that an appropriate federal function?

"OMB, in my opinion, is insisting that we break our own law in ordering such cuts. I refer to Section 7(b)(9) of the US Railroad Retirement Act of 1974 in quoting: 'The *Board shall maintain* such offices, provide such equipment, furnishing, supplies, services and facilities, and employ such individuals and provide for their compensation and expenses as may be necessary to the *proper discharge* of its function' (emphasis added).

"Congress gave the 'ball' to the Railroad Retirement Board, not to OMB. OMB personnel seem to think they know what is best for the railroad community, for they are taking the 'ball' from us and making a mockery of our law, and in so doing they usurp the will of Congress. Their game plan appears to be one of achieving their goal 'by hook or by crook,' and if Congress does not intervene soon, our system will collapse, and those we serve will be the ones who will suffer most.

"Please allow me to boast for a moment. The US Railroad Retirement Board is one of the most cost-efficient agencies in our government. For every dollar we pay out in retirement and disability benefits, less than eight tenths of one penny is spent on administrative costs. No other agency approaches that record of achievement. Every administrative penny comes out of our trust fund, and every penny in our trust fund comes from the railroad community. Isn't it reasonable to suggest that if the railroad community pays for our services, they should be given that which they have paid for?

"As stated so well in Senate Resolution 334, our administrative costs cannot alter the national debt nor affect the deficit in any real way—our administrative funds merely pass through the federal budget.

"It has often been said that the youth of our country represent our future. But we must never forget that the future is always carried in on the back of the past. We owe so much to our forefathers who fought for social justice and a better life. Now it is up to us to preserve and protect the interests of our elderly if we are to remain a great and noble nation. Thank you for listening, and, once again, thank you for inviting me to this hearing."

The response from the audience was overwhelming, including a standing ovation and prolonged applause. Within a week, the president's personally appointed inspector general appeared in my office unannounced. He was looking for a bureaucratic anarchist. Finding none, he returned to his office to file his report with the White House. Two weeks later the OMB personnel who had been handling the RRB forced reductions were reassigned to other duties. The dogs had been called off, and we were allowed to proceed without further interference from that administration.

A bureaucrat is often called upon to serve many masters. To whom does he or she owe the greatest allegiance—the public, the Congress, the president, or the law? It is best for all concerned, including the bureaucrat, always to follow those laws that are aimed at serving the common good.

Let us continue repeating "The Pledge," contemplating each word, thus supporting unity—with freedom and justice for all.